Québec

1850–1950

Québec

1850–1950

Photographs selected and with an introduction by

Lionel Koffler

FIREFLY BOOKS

A FIREFLY BOOK

Published by Firefly Books Ltd. 2005

First printing

Publisher Cataloging-in-Publication Data (U.S.)

Québec 1850-1950 / photographs selected and with an introduction by Lionel Koffler
[304] p. : col. photos. ;   cm.
Includes index.
Summary: A collection of archival photographs of life in Québec during the years 1850-1950.
ISBN 1-55407-041-4
1. Québec (Québec) — Pictorial works.
2. Québec (Québec) — History — Pictorial works. I. Koffler, Lionel. II. Title.
971.4/47104/0222 dc22   F1054.5.Q3LQ43   2005

Library and Archives Canada Cataloguing in Publication

Koffler, Lionel
Québec, 1850-1950 / photographs selected and with an introduction
by Lionel Koffler.

This publication is an anthology drawn from several books in the collection entitled *Aux limites de la mémoire*, the original French version of which is published by les Publications du Québec.
Includes index.
ISBN 1-55407-041-4

1. Québec (Province)—History—19th century—Pictorial works.
2. Québec (Province)—History—20th century—Pictorial works. 3. Québec (Province)—Social life and customs—19th century—Pictorial works.
4. Québec (Province)—Social life and customs—20th century—Pictorial works. I. Title.

FC2912.K64 2005 971.4'0022'2
C2005-903925-6

Published in the United States by
Firefly Books (U.S.) Inc.
P.O. Box 1338, Ellicott Station
Buffalo, New York 14205

Published in Canada by
Firefly Books Ltd.
66 Leek Crescent
Richmond Hill, Ontario L4B 1H1

Cover and interior design by Bob Wilcox

Printed in Canada

The publisher gratefully acknowledges the financial support for our publishing program by the Canada Council for the Arts, the Ontario Arts Council and the Government of Canada through the Book Publishing Industry Development Program.

HALF TITLE PAGE
WAITING PATIENTLY
Well-dressed young children stand on the wooden sidewalk. Rue Iberville, Rivière-du-Loup, circa 1905.

TITLE PAGE
A RIDE IN THE WOODS
This goat seems quite content to pull their light garden cart. Saint-Denis (Kamouraska), circa 1920.

FACING PAGE
AT REST
This old man in Saint-Pierre on the Île d'Orléans has earned his rest

Contents

Introduction

The pictures in this book were taken by many cameras and photographers over the course of a century. While the earliest of them were shot at the dawn of photography, the citizens of Québec were living in a society that was, by that time, already 300 years old.

It was a society that had persevered through the most difficult struggles, against constant and implacable enemies: the harsh weather, the unpredictable ocean, the endless forest and the loneliness of living in a vast landscape with none of our contemporary communication tools and methods.

Over those 300 years, people in Québec established communities, gained comfort from their faith and religion, raised big families and learned to live on the harvests from the land. If other regions of Canada were just beginning to be settled in the 1850s, all were on the cusp of a revolution in knowledge, communication and transportation that changed traditional ways of life forever.

It was a very tough life. Winters were long and summers very brief. While the fish were huge and abundant beyond our imagining, fishing boats were small and unreliable, and the dangers were many and fearsome. The rough comradeship of the mining and logging camps disguised the hazards of injury and death and the long separation of men and their families.

Like pioneers in all parts of the country, les Québecois persevered, becoming a close-knit and strong people, deeply rooted to the land and customs. The pictures in this book show people at their toil—ploughing land, harvesting grain, drying fish, milling lumber and flour and building homes and barns. But many of the barefoot boys on the farm are grinning at the camera; others, unaware of the photographer, are smiling as they chase chickens, gather maple sap or intently work on making wagon wheels with deep satisfaction in the quality of their craft. And there were always opportunities for celebration: weddings, travel, barn-raisings, newborn children.

The late 19th century was a time of change from traditional, agricultural hand-work, which lasted in some parts of Québec right through the 1950s, to the exciting industrial era, with its railways, telephones, trucks, steel bridges and airplanes. We turn from the flax-processing and ox-carts to the early wood-burning locomotives, from square-timber log rafts and sailing ships to Quebec City street railways; from birchbark teepees and canoes to the conservatories and vast gardens of the railroad barons' homes in Montreal.

Throughout, there is evidence of everyday ingenuity. The farmers had their own breeds of small, stocky and tough livestock — cattle and horses that could cope with the chilly climate and the mud. They used tree roots and cordwood for fences, built windmills to pump water and grind flour and combined European roof thatching with log and stone house materials to make sturdy homes.

Still, it was backbreaking work. Stones came up through the soil every spring and had to be moved to the fields' edges; forests could be cut, but the farmers still had to pull the stumps out of the muddy land using oxen and their own strength. Big families were a distinct asset, but the seigniorial system of dividing land among the offspring of farmers meant that many young men were forced off the farm. We see the sons here as a diverse group of tradesmen: wheelwright, miner, logger, ice-cutter, carpenter, sailor, cooper and fisherman. We see the daughters too, in their traditional roles: baking bread in massive outdoor ovens, spinning, weaving and teaching.

But the modern era that brought in the photographers arrived by train.

After the forests at the rivers' edges were felled, the railroad brought logs from the interior to the rivers. It moved the ore to smelters, crops to town and people to each other. The demands of building the railroads required engineers to design and build amazingly intricate trestles, the great viaduct at Cap Rouge and the Québec Bridge, once considered the eighth wonder of the world. The railroad made Montreal a city of great wealth and sophistication, we can see the splendour brought by railroad wealth: mansions, gardens, silks and estates.

Through accident or intent, most of the photographers' subjects are human in a setting: kids at school or helping out in the fields or with livestock, men and women in their gardens, at their workbenches, and in conversation. Details are telling: a young boy in a group shot is holding the paw of the family dog to keep it still. An old farmer and his wife both smoke pipes.

A scene from 1897, in a Montreal train station, shows nine people about to ascend a Pullman car. Most are white, the men with mutton-chop whiskers and waistcoats, and the women in many-layered dresses. All are leaning on sticks and chatting. The two bowler-hatted black men are slightly apart, their clothing simpler but superbly elegant.

The cover image is one of the most quietly descriptive. On a hillside in Saint-François, on the Île d'Orléans, an old cedar-rail fence separates a meadow from two houses and a barn across the road. All the structures are beautifully proportioned, their porches and door yards tidy and fruit trees flank them. The sun is shining on the whole scene, and in the foreground a couple are gazing proudly at their home and the horse that's prancing beside them. It is a scene of quiet beauty and simple pride that we are lucky to witness.

The grand homes of the early 20th century and their gardens were favourite subjects. The builders and owners were Allans, Prices, Morgans and Rosses, but also Prefontaines and Lafleurs. Conservatories and tropical gardens were the rage for a while, and monumental structures like Lord Strathcona's conservatory lasted into the 1940s. Others, such as the chateau-like prison for women and the Château Frontenac, are strongly memorable.

The photographers ranged from absolute amateurs with a family camera to journalists of the day, to the great William Notman. We are fortunate to have these images, which have been carefully collected for decades and often lovingly restored, and we are grateful to les Publications du Québec for their expertise and assistance in making this book possible.

These images give us a glimpse of 10 decades of tradition and change. While there are echoes of those traditions in New England and New Brunswick, and the changes were paralleled throughout North America, the combination and the timing are unique to Québec.

Lionel Koffler, 2005

THE PHOTOGRAPHS

POTATO PICKING

In the 1940s, many young people in eastern Québec set out in the fall to work for the commercial potato growers in New Brunswick. In some regions of Québec school holidays were scheduled during harvest season. The largest Québec producers also hired local workers. They were given a sturdy basket made from hardwood strips which, once full, was emptied into a wooden bushel or crate for shipment to the warehouse. This crew was probably less exuberant by the end of their long day!

13

BRINGING IN THE HAY
Resembling a slow-moving porcupine, the hay glides over the road
in Cap Tourmente, Montmorency, to the sound made by the wheel
hub hitting the axle. The driver occupies a first-class seat, allowing
him to admire the countryside and smell the cut grass. 1948.

HARVESTING THE FLAX

Flax has long been harvested by hand in order to obtain the longest fibres possible. On the farm of Émilien Babin in Caplan on the Gaspé Peninsula, the entire family participated in the harvest. The flax stems are spread out on the ground in long rows called swaths, where they are exposed to dew and the sun's rays for three or four weeks. This process, called retting, hardens the stems before the husk of the plant is broken and the fibre removed. 1948.

AN ABUNDANT HARVEST

A beautiful harvest is expected at this farm located in Ville-Marie in the Témiscamingue region. In the latter half of the 19th century, after many years of using the sickle, then the scythe, Québec farmers began to use machines to harvest oats. Initially, the harvester only cut the grain and left it in swaths. After 1875 an improved machine allowed the grain to be cut and bound in sheaths in one operation. The sheaths were left on the field to finish ripening before being stored in the barn.

◁ THE ROOT CELLAR

For years, farmers in Québec built root cellars to preserve their fruit and vegetables from the rigours of winter. Where the lay of the land permitted, the cellar was built close to the vegetable garden into the side of a slope, as shown on this farm in Saint-Donat. The walls were made of stone and the roof was covered with soil. 1942.

△ THE POTATO DIGGER

Farmers who produced food only for their families harvested potatoes using a plough to till the furrows and a garden hoe to remove the tubers. Commercial producers used a harvester pulled by two or three horses. The tubers were left to dry on the field before being stored. c. 1900

△ THE WOODSHED

During the 1950s, in Saint-Henri-de-Lévis and throughout the Québec countryside, houses were still heated with wood. In the summer, the split wood was stacked in the lean-to, the walls of which were often nothing more than a series of open arches for easy access.

▷ MILKING THE COWS

Milking was a familiar chore. The cows had to be brought back from the fields slowly because if they were made to run they would lose their milk. Milking a dozen cows by hand took an hour. The milk then had to be taken to the house or dairy to be put through the centrifuge before the farmer was finished. 1948.

△ SPRAYING THE ORCHARD

To fight scab, which attacked leaves and fruit during cool, wet summers, fruit trees were sprayed with a sulphur mist as soon as the leaves appeared. The process would be repeated twice more, once when the fruit buds were pink and once after the petals had fallen off the flowers. The horses were covered to protect them from the spray.

▷ THE PUBLIC MARKET

It's rush hour at the Champlain Market near the port of Quebec City, around 1910. Truck farmers, fruit sellers, bakers and other fresh-food merchants meet for another day of intense activity. These public markets gradually disappeared over the years.

MÉRITE AGRICOLE

The *Mérite agricole* competition was instituted in 1889. Each year, farmers competed for gold, silver and bronze medals in recognition of their efforts to improve their farms. Judges visited every farm and awarded each one a score. This photo shows the three judges of the 1909 competition accompanied by the director of a farm at Saint-Georges on Anticosti Island, which belonged to Henri Menier, a wealthy French chocolate producer.

THE LITTLE CANADIENNE
The Canadienne cow is descended from the earliest farm animals exported to New France and is considered the oldest cattle breed in North America. Small in size, the Canadienne is recognized for its hardiness and the high fat concentration in its milk, making it well suited to milk and cheese production. In 1883 it was estimated that 75 percent of the milk herd in Québec did not contain any foreign blood. Despite attempts to improve the breed, other breeds that produced more milk soon replaced the little Canadienne. 1943.

GATHERING HAY

Adoption of the mechanical loader represented an important step towards the complete mechanization of haymaking. Appearing at the end of the 19th century, this machine raked the hay and hoisted it over the slatted sides of the wagon. All that remained for the men to do was spread the hay evenly over the wagon bed using a pitchfork and stamp it down so that none was lost during the trip back to the barn. 1943.

SCREENING THE GRAIN

After the harvest, farmers had to screen the seeds for next season's planting to eliminate weed seeds, debris and seeds that were too small. A series of sieves with holes of different sizes would be bought communally, often by the agricultural or parish club. Before the introduction of screening machines, seeds had to be sorted by hand. 1942.

THE THATCHED ROOF

Early settlers brought the skills for making a thatched roof from Europe. This roof style was labour intensive, but it was also very economical because the materials were produced on the farm and the roof lasted a long time. Rafters were placed on wooden poles to which sheaths of straw were attached. The stems had to be well aligned by hand or by using a large comb. Each parish had two or three thatched roofs. This barn in Saint-Urbain was the last building in Charlevoix to have a thatched roof.

STUMPING

Stumping was by far the settlers' most tedious task. Help from family or neighbours was needed to drive the oxen while a hook was anchored to one large root at a time. Oxen are well adapted to this type of work because of their low centre of gravity; they just pull forward and the roots yield. However, the process had to be repeated several times to remove large stumps, and the settler had other jobs to do. This settler still has to finish the roof and foundation of his house. 1935.

△ THE WOOD SHOP

Hydroelectric power was still rare on Île aux Coudres but the islanders knew how to tame the wind. Flour mills, saw mills, threshers and other equipment outfitted with sails made of wooden boards and canvas drove a variety of machines. This photo shows the shop of a carpenter who took advantage of this free and abundant energy.

▷ THE CRADLE SCYTHE

Consisting of a scythe to which sticks of wood were attached, the cradle scythe allowed grain to be cut and sheathed in a single operation. The swaths were assembled using a rake to form sheaths that were bound with strips of red willow or reeds. The cradle scythe was gradually abandoned in favour of the mechanical harvester. In some regions, in particular the mountains of Charlevoix, some families still harvested their crops using this traditional method until the 1940s.

TAMING THE WIND

Windmills were very common in eastern Québec during the second half of the 19th century. Farmers knew how to take advantage of the winds that swept the shores of the St. Lawrence. The one shown here was located in Saint-Raphaël in Bellechasse county. It had an unusual number of spars outfitted with wooden boards and was used primarily to grind grain.

RAISING THE FRAME

Rural structures had long been built using large pieces of timber whose strength hadn't been calculated. Beginning in the 1920s, the Ministry of Agriculture supplied farmers with drawings prepared by experts. This allowed sturdier and more practical structures to be constructed. In this barn, the storage area under the roof is free of any obstructions. However, new construction techniques did not eliminate traditional rituals. This combination barn and cowshed, built around 1940, is raised with the help of relatives and neighbours. The fir tree on the last rafter indicates the end of this part of the work and the moment for all those who helped to sit down to a good meal.

A WOODEN PEN FOR THE HENS
This pen made of cordwood ensures that the white hen can no longer escape to the forest. The children have brought her a few bread crusts.

LAUNDRY

His sleeves rolled up, É. Simard heats the water that he has drawn from the lake. After soaping, rubbing and rinsing his laundry, he hangs it on the rope holding the tents. 1913.

THE FLAX BEE

Flax has been harvested and processed to produce a refined fabric for millennia. The flax is uprooted in the fall and, after several stages of drying and ripening, the stem is broken to remove the fibre that will ultimately be spun. This work was generally carried out by women who worked together during a bee like this one, circa 1910.

WEAVING WOOL

The weaving loom was often set up in the attic over the summer kitchen because of the space it required. In the past, each farm had all the necessary tools to process wool: a spinning wheel, a bobbin-bank, a lifter reel, a reel and a weaving loom. In this July 1925 photo, Marie-Louise Dumont is weaving wool blankets.

THE FIRST STEP

Assembling the weaving loom required several hours of work. Preparing the warp beam was the first step. The yarn, first held between two large wooden pegs, was measured according to the number of items to be woven on the loom and their measurements. Passing the yarn between the linen blades was a true test of patience. In case of a mistake, everything had to be taken apart and work had to begin again. 1925.

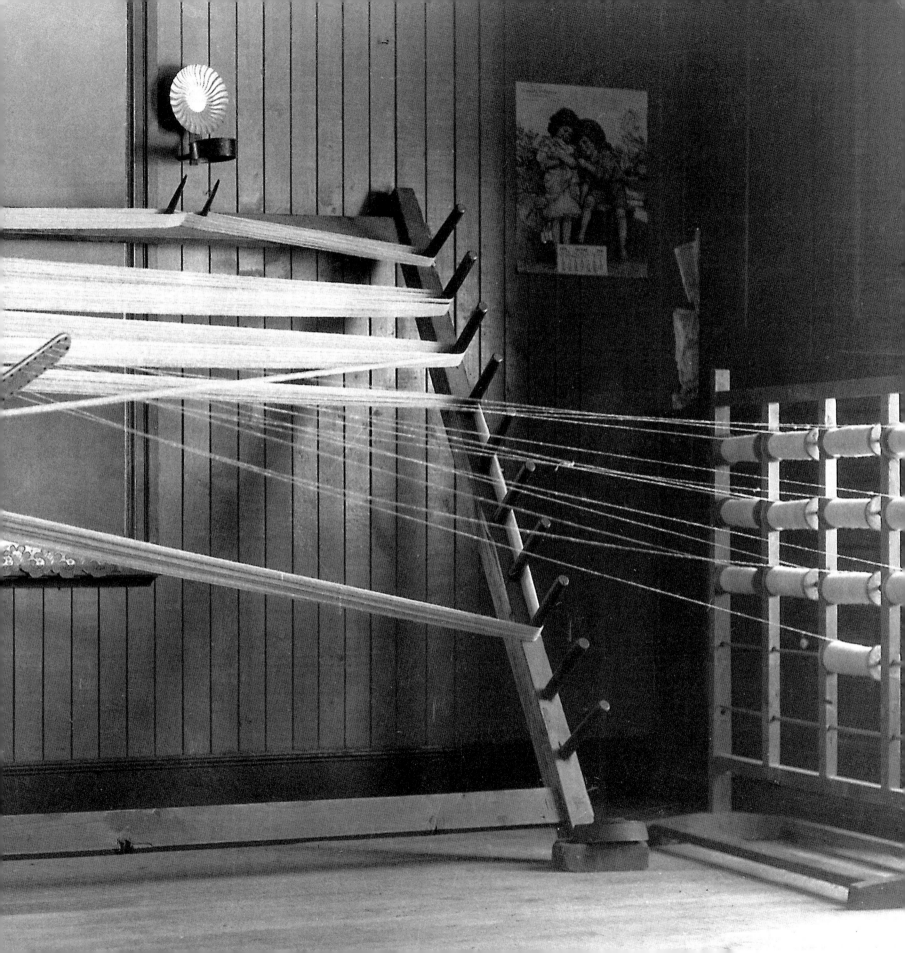

◁ **LEARNING TO SEW**

Learning how to sew and do handicrafts for the home began at an early age; between the ages of eight and nine, a girl learned the simplest braiding and weaving techniques, often passed on directly by her grandmother, who lived under the same roof.

△ **INSIDE THE HOUSE**

A stovepipe runs along the ceiling; a white ceramic stove is polished to a shine, its plate-warmers and shaving mirror above, and its kettle always at hand to make some tea. The sitting room for receiving visitors is at the back through the archway; in it sits a piano, a vase and the best rocking chairs. The black cross of temperance adorns one wall and everywhere, the waxed linoleum gleams as if new. The lady of the house abandoned her spinning wheel during the time it took to take the picture.

△ THE FUTURE

Making the most of a beautiful day, this grandmother in Sainte-Brigitte-de-Laval has taken her spinning wheel just outside the door and efficiently spins the spring wool. A young mother knits something for her youngest child while trying to make him sleep, her foot poised on the base of the cradle.

▷ ON THE SWING

Between these giant trees with powerful and firmly anchored roots, little children in Sainte-Brigitte-de-Laval innocently play.

SANDY-BAY, QUE.

◁ SUNDAY BEST

Large families were required to help work the land. In 1943, 10 years
after settling in Sainte-Anne-de-Roquemaure, the Ludger Dionne family
had 15 children who posed proudly in their Sunday clothes in front of
the modest home. It is hard to believe that the women of that era could
raise so many children, even if the older girls helped take care of the
younger children.

△ LIGHTHOUSE OF THE SOUL

Beautiful in their simplicity, these little churches dotted the banks of
the St. Lawrence. Built on the river embankments, they represented a
lighthouse devoted to the souls of villagers and sailors alike. More like a
big house than a small temple, these places of worship were often the
only public buildings and meeting places. This photo of the Baie-des-
Sables church is a reminder of a not-so-distant time when the number
of steeples was counted, not the number of villages. c. 1910.

◁ **SILVER WEDDING ANNIVERSARY**

The Hôpital Saint-Joseph-du-Précieux-Sang, the oldest hospital in all of eastern Québec, celebrates its 25th anniversary in 1914. The crowd is attending mass—the men are holding their hats in their hands—in front of a nicely decorated altar set up outside the hospital.

△ **A WELL-EARNED REST**

In the evening in Malbaie. this man and woman sit on their veranda. She has taken out her wheel to spin a little in the last rays of the sun. He, wearing a pea jacket, warms his old bones in silence, religiously puffing on his pipe. Friends for life and now companions on the last leg of their journey together, this couple has worked hard before arriving at the peace that comes with age.

BAKING BREAD

These women bake bread for the week in Saint-Urbain. Given the length
of the oven and the 48 loaves that it can hold, this must be a large
family. Since settlement began, the outdoor bread oven was an essential
feature of most homes. Built on loam, the oven was covered with sheets
of bark or untrimmed planks, or later with sheet metal, as in this photo,
to protect it from inclement weather. Some wealthier habitants owned
an indoor bread oven, located adjacent to the hearth, while poorer ones
baked their bread in the stove oven or even in a cauldron.

OUR DAILY BREAD

Madame Marie Dumont is busy making homemade bread under the watchful eye of her grandson, who moulds his own bread in a little pan. Bread was generally baked in an oven located outside, but in the winter the oven of the kitchen stove was used. More than a simple, weekly chore, this task took on a double meaning, for bread was both a dietary staple and symbolized the holy bread, which they piously received each Sunday at the communion table. 1926.

◁ **THE SNYDER HOUSE**

We know little of the Snyder house but we cannot help but succumb to its charm. Built in the Queen Anne style, inspired by late 17th century England, the house has a steep roof, oriel and dormer windows and elaborate chimneys, veranda and awnings. 1894.

△ **THE SPORTS CAR**

Early in Québec's history, the King of France sent several dozen mares and a few stallions for distribution to the gentlemen of the colony. The Canadian breed, which evolved from these first animals, has a short body, massive hooves and long hair. This is the horse depicted in the paintings of Cornelius Krieghoff. This photo, which dates from 1866, shows Aigle gris, one of the Canadian stallions at the École d'agriculture de Sainte-Anne-de-la-Pocatière, pulling a buggy with a folding top, the sports car of its day! 1866.

DRIED COD

Once the undried, salted cod had been spread out on fish flakes in the sun for six to eight days and turned twice, it was stacked in salt piles in the open air and covered during the night. The result was cod as dry as a cedar shingle and ready for the market.

AVENUE ROYALE

This photo shows an old stone house covered in pargeting, in the Breton style, with a heavy, steeply sloping roof over rooms lit through dormer windows and a large attic that served no practical purpose. This type of construction with its deep rooms did not allow much light to enter, and the fireplace that backs onto the gable wall did little to heat all the rooms. Montmorency, circa 1920.

TRAVELLING SALESMAN

A travelling salesman offers his wares to a woman in Saint-Rosaire d'Arthabaska. The salesman knew how to charm his customers, even the young ones. He restocked his inventory with frequent trips to the manufacturers and brought new things to families who rarely had a chance to go to the city to shop. 1957.

LABOUR DAY

A trade wagon at Labour Day celebrations in 1895 carries on a tradition that began under French rule and was inherited from the *Compagnons du Tour de France*. This society, dedicated to teaching the manual trades in France, saw many of its practices passed on in Québec.

CLEAR-CUTTING

A graveyard of tree stumps capped with snow, around 1910. As far as the eye can see, nature has conceded to the unceasing advance of the clear-cutting practice, which takes all the wood from the forest. Loggers had been cutting here for about 20 years. Once the mountain is completely denuded, there will be no other choice but to move elsewhere and begin again.

SNOWFALL, 1919

While the adults are busy digging out the doors, windows and steps, the baby is muffled up using warm, soft furs. Propped up in its sleigh, this baby might just remember its first winter and the endless, fluffy whiteness of snow.

△ ICE

A capstan was built on the edge of the St. Lawrence River, at Gifford, to extract pieces of ice, which would then be preserved in sawdust. They would be cut and delivered door-to-door all year long on the streets of Quebec City. 1949.

▷ AIR CONDITIONING

Early air conditioning was fairly primitive. Large blocks of ice were used to cool the air piped to first-class coaches and dining cars. Ice was also required to keep food cool in the kitchen car. The blocks were cumbersome. Here, employees load the ice in the Glen Yard before the train wheels into Windsor Station to collect its passengers. 1946.

WINTER WORK

In winter, when they could not work the land, farmers cut wood to sell in the village. They stood the tree trunks upright to avoid finding them covered with snow just when they were ready to be cut for firewood. 1950.

A WINTER SHORTCUT
Farmers on the Île d'Orléans used a winter road over the frozen
St. Lawrence River. The tops of fir trees served as markers indicating
the route to follow after a snowstorm. This winter scene resembles
those painted by Krieghoff 125 years earlier. 1949.

◁ **A VILLAGE SCHOOL**

    Looming over the village landscape in Saint-Pierre on the Île d'Orléans at
the end of the 19th century, this type of architecture borrowed the shape
of a simple house with an extension added at the front. A window in
the Palladian style allows light into the attic and a large classroom. This
uncommon architectural style is found primarily in a few villages in eastern
Québec, such as Saint-Alexandre in Kamouraska county.

△ **THE LITTLE ENGLISH CLASS**

    On this day in Saint-Pierre on the Île d'Orléans, Mrs. Driscoll, who teaches
English to the young children of the parish, warned them to put on their
best clothes for the photographer's visit. The boys are on one side, wearing
their knee socks and jacket, the girls on the other, in their pretty dresses with
bows in their hair. And everyone is sitting up straight.

◁ ON THE WAY TO SCHOOL

When you walked to school in bare feet, as these children in Sainte-Émilie, Lotbinière, are doing, children wearing shoes would step on your toes. When walking on gravel roads you had to avoid the sharp stones, and in the fields, the cow pats.

△ YOUNG ADULTS

These boys, around 1928, are wearing an armband on their left arm and a white bow decorated with a chalice and a gold fringe. The candle and the diploma that they are holding attest to their successful completion of the Little Catechism taught by the parish priest.

A UNIQUE TEAM
Considered man's best friend, these dogs were devoted and loyal servants. Harnessed to a sled in winter and a cart in summer, they also chased the cows in the field, protected the farm and prevented the children from going on the road. An inestimable partner in all games, the brave animals patiently acquiesced to the whims of their young masters. c. 1930.

PREFERENTIAL TREATMENT

This young girl in Saint-François-de-Montmagny is busy taking care of a beautiful grey horse that seems to be enjoying the plate of oats she is holding out to him. The girl is saving some dry hay for later. 1946.

PRIDE OF PLACE

Clean and well-maintained homes built to last; good, fertile soil that drains quickly and a frisky filly that carries its head high and will be the most beautiful horse pulling the Sunday carriage must have all given great pleasure to this man and woman in Saint-François on the Île d'Orléans.

△ **GIDDY-UP**
Two boys enjoy a horseback ride while the hay wagon returns from the fields in Sainte-Geneviève-de-Batiscan.

▷ **PAPA'S BIG HORSE**
A farmer's son has his first riding lesson in Saint-Paul-de-Chester, Arthabaska.

AUTUMN PLOUGHING

The harvest has been brought in and the farmer is preparing the land for seeding in the spring. The point of the plough carves the soil the length of a perfectly straight furrow while the horses steadily and forcefully move forward. The man firmly grips the handles and casts an eye from time to time on the two children playing in their bare feet in the freshly turned soil. c. 1930.

THE MIRROR

Nature featured prominently in the world of photographer Jean-Baptiste Dupuis. In this picture, circa 1910, nature, sometimes wild, sometimes tame, serves as a backdrop for a small group of people, in Sunday dress, who provide a sense of scale. Lakes and rivers fascinated Dupuis: their surface reflected the light, like a mirror, creating a magical atmosphere.

GRANDFATHER

Grandfathers talk about the weather and the coming harvest, tell tales of their youth and predict the future. Grandsons listen closely as traditions, tales, legends, beliefs and ancestral values are passed on. And one fine day, the child will be surprised to hear himself say, "My grandfather used to say…" 1925.

◁ **THE OLD JESUIT MILL**
   Solidly built from masonry and coated with pargeting, the Jesuits' mill
   captured the water from the Lorette River in Ancienne-Lorette. Built
   in 1755, it was used until the 1950s by generations of farmers who
   processed their grain into fine wheat flour and meal.

△ **CLEARING THE ROCKS**
   Every year, rocks that were forced to the surface by the frost in this field
   in Saint-Rosaire d'Arthabaska were collected in the spring and moved
   out of the way of the plough. 1952.

SETTLER

Willie Duval from Île Bonaventure is one of the descendants of the Gauls who put down roots on the shores of Gaspé. Mocking and mischievous, cheerful and confident in their strength, these tough fellows came to fish and decided to stay.

LOADING HAY

Fieldhands in Rivière-des-Prairies demonstrate that loading hay so that it won't fall off along the way is an art form: first prepare four good corners, then point each pitchfork load of hay along the sides, then comb the load before leaving the field. There is nothing better than the traditional way. 1950.

THE CANADIAN HOUSE

This familiar shape was built around 1910. The curved roof punctuated by several dormer windows that allowed light into the bedrooms; the large, elevated veranda and the two floors situated well above ground all indicate how Québec homes were adapted to a harsh climate. Referred to as a "maison canadienne," this structure often housed a business as well as a family residence, as shown by the second entrance located on the side of the house.

A VISIT TO THE FARM
Tiny Marie-Anna, wearing her best clothes, is visiting the neighbouring farm. Caught between two large pigs that she is stroking as if they were kittens, she doesn't appear to be frightened. 1907.

FAMILY LIFE

Homes for the elderly are a recent phenomenon. On this farm, circa 1910, grandparents lived with their children and grandchildren. Adding an addition to the house often made it possible to accommodate everyone on ancestral land.

ADDING CLAY TO THE SOIL

Sandy soils suffer from excessive permeability. The farmers of Saint-Raymond de Portneuf addressed the problem by spreading clay on their land. Clay does not enhance fertility the way chemical fertilizers do, but by retaining the water in the soil, it helps the soil absorb nutrients. c. 1900.

AN ESSENTIAL SERVICE
Before the iron band is wrapped around the wheel, each spoke has to be in place along the rim. The wheelwright was as essential to rural life as the blacksmith and the farrier.

△ THE SQUARE BARN

Like the octagonal barn, the square barn reflects American influence. This type of structure was found primarily in the Eastern Townships, built by immigrants from New England. With a central campanile that served as a ventilation shaft, its imposing drawbridges and tiny windows, this structure in Farnham looks more like a medieval fortress than a farm building in the Québec countryside. Also distinctive is its flat roof, which is poorly adapted to winter in Québec.

▷ STORING CREAM

This well in Saint-Barthélemy, Berthier, was the best place for keeping cream cool while waiting to take it to the butter-making factory. Pots of fresh meat purchased on Fridays from the travelling butcher were also kept in the well for weekend meals.

◁ **MAPLE SAP**
His mouth on the wooden spout, a boy tries to determine which maple is producing the sweetest sap. c. 1900.

△ **MAPLE SAP CARRIER**
Ever since Aboriginal peoples taught the settlers of New France how to make maple syrup, Quebeckers have never stopped "harvesting maples" in the spring. The farmer would attach two wooden buckets to a yoke placed over his shoulders, then go to collect the precious liquid that flowed into the spruce troughs. This task was less onerous when an ox or a horse pulled the barrel that would gradually be filled with sap. c. 1900.

SPRING

In spring, the yoke is lighter and connoisseurs will tell you that the maple syrup in Petite-Rivière-Saint-François has a taste and a golden colour that are unparalleled. The women here are wearing their most beautiful cotton aprons for harvesting the maples.

92

THE BARREL

The horse pulling the barrel of maple syrup would stop on its own when it saw a person with a full bucket; once it heard the syrup poured into the barrel, the horse would set off again. This photograph, taken in L'Ange-Gardien, will bring back memories to those who were lovers at that time. 1947.

△ SUGAR SEASON

At this time of year in Ironside in the Ottawa Valley, it was rare to harness two horses to the maple syrup barrel since the snow was melting and the paths were difficult. When a horse became stuck in the mud, it twisted from side to side until it could find hard snow, risking injury to the other horse.

▷ THE TRADITIONAL WAY, IN LOTBINIÈRE

Before the advent of distilleries, maple taffy and sugar were produced in a big cauldron suspended from a bracket over a fire. Before the Europeans brought metal containers, Aboriginal peoples produced a sweet drink by throwing hot stones in a birchbark container filled with maple sap. 1950.

94

STURDY FELLOWS

About 15 men chopped down the spruce trees needed to build this new engineering office. All construction materials were found on site, with no question of sawing, planing and painting. Logs were fine. When the foreman shouted "Lift!" the men raised the already notched logs and sited them. It took two weeks to build the structure. 1913.

△ THE STONE WEEDER

Small stones could easily be carried out of the field but this was not the case for large rocks. In this instance, a "stone weeder" was necessary, that is, a capstan on wheels. Two horses hold the winch in place while the other two pull the cables of the notched pulley, which is used to hoist the rock. Once raised, the rock can be placed on the edge of the field. 1945.

▷ GREEN FODDER

The possibility of storing fodder in silos revolutionized the Québec dairy industry. Preserving green hay (clover, alfalfa, etc.) or chopped corn in silos allowed farmers to improve the feeding of their herds during winter, thereby producing milk over the entire year. Earlier, cows could only be fed dried hay or straw during winter stabling; butter- and cheese-producing plants had to suspend their operations until the cows returned to pasture. These first wooden stave silos were held together using steel cables, similar to old barrels. 1949.

△ LEEK STEMS

The leek is a tuberous, edible plant commonly found in Québec. While it is growing, the tops of the leaves are cut off and the seedling is covered with mulch to allow a fair-sized white stem to be harvested in the fall. Since leeks do not freeze, they can be preserved under snow during winter. Commercial producers bound the pre-washed stems in bunches, which are then packed in crates to be shipped to market. 1946.

▷ A RUSTIC GRADER

The first factories producing farm implements began operating in the middle of the 19th century, but farmers continued to produce some of their own tools. This resident of the Trois-Rivières region is using a primitive grader to level his field. 1944.

△ THE LITTLE CART

Made on the farm, except for the wheels, which were purchased at the wheelwright, this little cart was used to transport firewood, sacks of mash and cans of milk or cream. On occasion, it was used as a toy when the youngest children were pulled along by their older siblings. Some models were designed to be pulled by a big dog, but the carts were usually pulled by hand. These two young boys in Beaumont are transporting a milk can from the farm to the side of the road where the truck from the dairy will pick it up.

▷ THE GRASS CUTTERS

Ewes have very good appetites and eat the weeds in the fields that the other farm animals disregard. When these ewes went to pasture, the farmer took care to place a wooden stanchion around their neck to prevent them from climbing through the fence. In Québec, sheep were raised mostly for their wool.

△ THE LONG CLIMB

Less than 15 years after the construction of the island bridge, the road to Saint-Pierre on the Île d'Orléans still appears to be very narrow and unsuitable for automobile traffic. The islanders had not yet changed their pace of life and were still fond of their ox carts. The animals were not fast, but they travelled far and cost almost nothing to feed.

▷ THE QUÉBEC HIGHLANDS

Irish and Scottish immigrants must have felt quite at home when they settled in the mountainous townships of northern Québec in the first half of the 19th century. High mountains, dark forests, green valleys, stone walls, sheep and the little shepherd wearing knee socks; all that's missing is the sound of a bagpipe air. This photo shows Tewkesbury, and the boy's name is Ross Heitshu.

GARDEN GATE

Few gates possess more charm than this one at the entrance to Mayor Mayberry's property on Aylmer Road in Aylmer. The gate combines French and Moorish motifs, an exotic combination of the fleur-de-lis and the crescent moon. Alymer Road was once home to the grand residences of lumber barons. The avenue of stately trees has fallen to make way for a four-lane highway, but the ambassadorial residences and golf courses still enjoy privileged views of the Ottawa River.

THE GARDEN

The Price family is synonymous with Québec's forest industry. The founder of the dynasty, William Price, is known as the Father of the Saguenay for his role in developing the region's vast strands of timber. His descendants built Price Brothers into one of the largest lumber and paper companies in the world. In the early 1920s, William's grandson, Sir William Price, built a residence in Kenogami, where he had established a newsprint mill. Tragically, he was killed in a landslide in 1924. After his death, his son moved into the family home, developing the garden begun by his father. 1925.

◁ **QUEBEC CITY**
In the early morning only deliverymen bringing milk, ice and bread are climbing the Côte d'Abraham to the Upper Town, Quebec City. Soon, tramways carrying office workers will appear on the rue de la Couronne, while others who have finished their night jobs will descend to the Lower Town.

△ **EARLY POLICE CAR**
At the end of the 19th century, residents of Montreal reported seeing cars that travelled without the help of a horse! No one suspected how much congestion this new means of transportation would cause on streets that were not designed for an invention that would soon be available to all.

△ ON THE WATER

During a beautiful summer's day, the natural harbours scattered along the length of the St. Lawrence drew many ladies and gentlemen onto the water. A few hours spent in the middle of the river allowed one to forget the worries of city life. With women and children admiring the view, men rowed and paddled them back to shore safe and sound. 1910.

▷ VELOCIPEDE

The first riders of the velocipede could be found in small circuses, causing the crowds to cry out by pretending to fall. Here and there, men drawn by the challenge of remaining perched on two wheels rode in parades during public celebrations.

IN GOOD COMPANY

One can learn much about people by examining the inside of their home. Many things in this photograph indicate that this is a relatively well-to-do home: the wallpaper, the large mirror, the armchairs and the many photographs. In good company, these two women prefer to pose in their own home rather than in the studio, an uncommon practice at the time. c. 1910.

112

ADIEU

Even in this modest home, as seen by the plain boards on the wall, nothing is spared to say farewell to the youngest child. The lace and bedding surrounding the infant shows that it has been wrapped in the most beautiful clothes. The candle and crucifix prove that, even if its time on earth was brief, everything possible was done for its soul. This scene, difficult for our eyes to look at, was part of daily life. It took until the middle of the century before there was any noticeable improvement in infant mortality. c. 1905.

113

Δ THE TIMES ARE CHANGING

Children have always loved to dress up. In the photo on the left, the clothes recall the "olden days" of the 1800s. Sitting side by side, the children are posing as their parents did, or even their grandparents. In the photo on the right, we see the changes in behaviour made by the 1920s: short hair for the girl, a casual suit for the boy and a relaxed attitude. Without a doubt, the times are changing.

▷ J.K.L. ROSS HOUSE

Like many of the houses in Montreal's Square Mile that have escaped demolition, the J.K.L. Ross house is now part of the campus of McGill University. It was built for Ross as a present from his father, James Ross, who had made his fortune as one of the main contractors on the construction of the Canadian Pacific Railway. The Rosses were interested in gardens. The garden was destroyed by road construction. 1926.

CORPUS CHRISTI

Having left the church, the procession gathers momentarily in front of the richly-adorned household altar to receive, in a dignified manner, the holy sacrament. Overhead, obedient girls, honoured to be taking part in such an event, personify the angels descended from heaven. The Sunday on which Corpus Christi is celebrated represents an important moment in the liturgical year. Like a king, the priest bearing the monstrance moves forward, covered by a canopy solemnly held by four churchwardens. 1919.

PLAYING CHECKERS

Dressed warmly and sporting the long beard of the elderly, grandfather clenches his pipe between his teeth. The little girl leans studiously on the checkerboard. They have opened the curtains to allow in more light or the day's warmth as young and old spend a precious moment together in Malbaie.

MAKING A GARDEN

Making a garden is long, laborious work. The Frères de l'instruction chrétienne et la Pointe-du-Lac believed that physical work was as much a part of school as textbooks and lessons. Students and teachers here work together to clear the stumps, the first stage in building their garden. c. 1940.

◁ **THE LITTLE PATH**
Elsie Reford was an amateur gardener without any formal training in horticulture. In the winter months she read gardening books and corresponded with other gardeners. She also studied the landscape carefully. Here, she created a path traversing the stream and leading up the hill on the other side. The boulders were replaced every spring, returned to their original position after being shifted downstream by the winter ice and spring floods. c. 1935.

▷ **URBAN PARADISE**
Soon after Hugh Allan added a conservatory to Ravenscrag, his opulent home on Mount Royal, his brother Andrew followed suit and added this conservatory to his Peel Street mansion. The Allans were one of the most powerful families in Montreal, owners of the Allan Line, the principal link between Montreal and Britain. The brothers began a trend that would see conservatories built on most of the mansions in Montreal's Square Mile. 1871.

SUMMER BOUNTY
　　Gardening has always been a favorite pastime in Québec. The Miller garden in Montreal contained both flowers and vegetables. 1896.

TEA

Kildonan Hall was the home of Robert MacKay, a merchant and senator, who was one of the directors of the Montreal Horticultural Society. Behind the palazzo-style house at the corner of Sherbrooke and Redpath streets was a large garden. In this photograph, Mrs. MacKay and her friend enjoy tea in the garden. 1895.

◁ THE CONSERVATORY

The conservatory of the George Stephen residence on Drummond Street was
a magnificent room in wrought iron and glass. After Stephen's brother-in-law
Robert Meighen occupied the house, the conservatory was opened to the public to
show off his collection of orchids. But by the time Meighen's daughter, Elsie, built
her own Montreal home, the fashion of building conservatories had passed. She
chose instead to garden in nature, building a garden on the estate left her by her
uncle, George Stephen, now commonly known as Les Jardins de Métis. 1884.

△ NOTRE-DAME-DES-NEIGES

Montreal's Roman Catholic cemetery was established on the sloping fields of Mount
Royal in 1853. Notre-Dame-des-Neiges was laid out by Henri-Maurice Perrault and
generations of architects and landscape architects have since participated in its
design. This photograph shows the cemetery's charnier, or dead-house, at the top
of a heavily landscaped walk in the early years of the cemetery. 1910.

VICTORIAN INFLUENCE
Victorian exuberance is everywhere in evidence in this house and garden. Located in Longueuil on the south shore of the St. Lawrence River, the garden of the Lusher residence is a hodgepodge of styles where croquet and contemplation both have their place. 1869.

PLAYING HOUSE

Fernande and Paul-Édouard are playing in the garden. Mama is
absorbed in her knitting, while Papa is smoking his pipe and resting
after a hard day. From a young age, children identify with their parents
and mimic the actions and mannerisms they observe and record. 1921.

◁ **THE POND**

The pond was intended as the central feature of the gardens landscaped by surveyor and architect John Ostell when he designed the Grand Séminaire building in 1855. Captured by a multitude of photographers, the pond also appears in the work of artists Clarence Gagnon and Adrien Hébert. This photograph captures the mystery and beauty of this remarkable urban space. The dome of the motherhouse of the Sœurs de la Congrégation Notre-Dame (now Dawson College) can be seen in the distance.

△ **ADVICE**

The dog seems to be in a great hurry to continue on its way, oblivious to the fact that its young master is receiving advice from the priest.

△ AT THE STORE

The simple counter made of wooden boards, the rudimentary bench, and the brick chimney propped up on the cabinet all make it clear that this is a small, local store offering a few necessities, as well as tobacco.

▷ THE CITY

Although the streets are still paved with cobblestones, Montreal had clearly grown into a major city by the 1930s.

◁ **THE WHEELWRIGHT**
The village wheelwright manufactured and repaired the wheels of all wagons and carts in Saint-Fidèle, Charlevoix. To ensure that the spokes were well anchored in the hub and rim of the wheel, the iron band was put in place while still red hot; upon cooling, it contracted and held the entire assembly together. 1942.

△ **THE FIRST CATERER**
Hetherington's Bakery, like most businesses in Quebec City in the early 20th century, advertised in English. Hetherington, a master baker, produced and distributed bread, cookies, cupcakes and wedding cakes.

SWEEPER

When electric street railways were introduced to Canada in the 1890s, it was generally assumed that they could run in the summers only. The Ottawa Electric Railway Company pioneered the use of sweeper cars to clear the tracks and keep them free of ice and snow. To make the streetcars usable in winter, the car's floor was covered with straw and stoves were added, thereby assuring the passengers' comfort. The street railway companies in Montreal and Quebec City followed suit. By 1903, Montreal had 19 sweeper cars.

OBSERVATION CAR

A feature of Montreal's street railways was the observation cars. Ornately decorated, they were a popular attraction and inspired local residents to put on their Sunday best for a family excursion to admire the sights. A monumental station hotel, Viger Station was where trains arrived and departed for Quebec City. Designed by American architect Bruce Price, who also designed the Château Frontenac, it was one of the most visible symbols of the Canadian Pacific's presence in Montreal. 1905.

HEALTHY ENTERTAINMENT
In the 1930s, clerics did not remove their cassocks except to sleep. This garment was not the most convenient for playing sports but these priests seem to be enjoying themselves skiing just the same.

IN A LEAGUE OF THEIR OWN

Sport, like many other activities in the 1920s, was largely the preserve of men. Despite this, some young women, often from well-to-do and educated backgrounds, were highly successful in creating women's hockey teams. These brave young women maintained their femininity and good manners as shown by the elegance of their pose.

△ A LITTLE GARDEN

Cleveland Morgan called his garden a "Lilliputian affair," but in fact it covered more than ten acres. He built this rock garden in a valley created by the construction of a high stone wall made to protect the garden from spring floods. There he had a large collection of alpine plants, nestled into crevasses between limestone boulders brought from adjacent fields. 1919.

▷ THE ART OF THE GARDEN

Hudson is one of Québec's oldest garden communities. Eugène Lafleur first built this residence in Hudson Heights in 1912 to the designs of Edward Maxwell. The grounds were designed by landscape architect Ormiston Roy, gardener of the Mount Royal Cemetery. Lafleur was a prominent Montreal lawyer and professor of law at McGill. These photographs were taken for the Law family in the 1920s after they acquired the property from the Lafleurs.

◁ THE HAGUE GARDEN

Montreal gardeners followed the trends and fashions at the turn of the 20th century just as they do today. Many new species were introduced to horticulture from the colonial outposts of Britain, France, Spain, Portugal and the Netherlands. Plants from subtropical climates, such as the Begonia, native to the Andes of Peru and Bolivia, flourished in Canadian summers. In the Hague garden, we see one of the favourites of the Victorian era, the castor oil plant, *Ricinus communis*, native to Africa. In addition to producing an oil used as a laxative, the plant's seeds are toxic. 1911.

△ HOUSE OF DREAMS

A garden is a fragile thing. Like too many of the creators of Québec's gardens, Hugh Paton made no provision for the continuation of his work. His house and property were sold after his death. Along with much of the land in Saraguay and environs, Paton Island has been developed for housing. The fate of Hugh Paton's garden should give pause for reflection. Conserving a garden is at least as difficult as creating one. c. 1921.

STEAMSHIP

With each arrival of the steamships, people crammed onto the pier to greet the visitors and to take them, by horse-drawn carriage, through the village to the hotel, explaining the local history along the way. Well-known and lesser-known personalities alike arrived by river, not to mention all kinds of goods and all the news. 1890.

MONTREAL DRY DOCK COMPANY

Noble without being pretentious, several examples of this type of yacht, built in the 1930s, have survived to today. Made from mahogany, they were highly polished as witness to the success of their owners. Each boat's magnificent hull consisted of powerful lines that married the shine of the varnish with the blaze of the brass.

IN THE WOODS
Under an exhausting sun, a team of horses struggles along. The unstripped logs dig into the dirt as they slide along and become clogged with sand and gravel.

THE TELEPHONE

The first businesses to take advantage of telephone service were primarily hotels and large companies. But Alexander Graham Bell's invention became increasingly affordable and the network had to be expanded to include new subscribers scattered around the province. The poles to hold the wires would gradually transform the landscape along country roads. c. 1930.

◁ **RUE SAINT-JEAN**

In the middle of the cobblestone street, metallic grooves on which the horse-drawn tramway travelled were also used by carters and delivery men whose vehicles were equipped with wheels that slotted into the grooves. Thus, they could calmly move about contrary to those who drove over the uneven stones.

THE PUMP

Δ In 1895, in Quebec City and Montreal, the steam pump used to fight fires was powered by a wood-burning or coal-burning boiler. Just like the other vehicles that followed along behind it bringing the ladders, hoses, axes and buckets, it was placed on a sled or a cart and pulled by high-spirited horses eager to run.

LAST RIDE

Fall is coming to a close; the snow has not yet arrived, but it won't be long. Barren trees line the streets that look a little sad under a grey sky. No matter, as little Paul Driscoll takes a final trip on his bicycle with Jonathan before trading in his wheels for his skates for many long months to come.

THE PETIT SÉMINAIRE DE QUÉBEC

Discrete and almost obliterated by the buildings surrounding it – the
basilica on the right and the chapel on the left – the main entrance
of the Petit Séminaire de Québec is indicated by two stone pillars. The
classical façade overtop the covered passageway and the rounded corner
façade of the Banque provinciale constitute one of the most famous
urban landscapes of the old capital.

◁ **MERCHANTS**

Merchants on both sides of rue Saint-Jean in Quebec City grab customers as they stroll along the wide, wooden sidewalks. Located on opposite sides of the street, the shops shown have been part of the landscape for decades: the grocer, J.A. Moisan, the shoe store, Joseph Demers, and the lingerie seller Giguère, better known as "Giguère's girls."

△ **THE RAILWAY**

Railways were a man's domain. Until the Second World War, few women worked for the railways, even in secretarial occupations. The young men in this office use typewriters and carbon paper. Their sleeves are held up with armbands, keeping their cuffs away from the ink and grime. Shipping goods by train required reams of paper: bills of lading, receipts, invoices and statements of accounts. The accounting systems were remarkably complex, with shipments either prepaid on the consignor's account or payable on delivery. 1901.

ST. CHRISTOPHER

The history of a nation is punctuated with traditions, which often derive from other traditions. Québec annals reveal that, from very early on, horse-drawn carriages were blessed in towns and villages. Naturally, this ritual was adapted to the automobile. On the last day of July when the feast of St. Christopher, patron saint of drivers, was celebrated, these gleaming automobiles in Rivière-du-Loup, all polished and spruced up, await the end of high mass. 1929.

LAURIER ET LA VICTOIRE

CONSACRÉ MA VIE A L'UNITÉ CANADA

POLITICS

Political life has always stirred the hearts of Québeckers. At a time before mass media, public meetings were often the only way to decide which candidate to vote for. The visit of a party leader could, at any time, provoke a large meeting. Wilfrid Laurier, seen sitting behind the lower banner, listens closely to a supporter's speech. This electoral campaign, which focused on free trade with the United States, would be the political legacy of Sir Wilfrid Laurier. c. 1910.

153

◁ HELLO!

This oversized telephone, something between a toy and an advertisement, with its crank, double bell, receiver and earphone, is fascinating. The telephone was introduced in rural Québec in the first quarter of the 20th century. Cities had already taken advantage of this new technology by the end of the 19th century. c. 1915.

△ SWITCHBOARD

Rapid technological change, like the installation of the telephone network, led to the creation of new types of employment, often held by women. Numerous telephone switchboards resembling this one were built where the operators, sitting on simple stools, manually established connections between different subscribers. c. 1930.

155

◁ FASCINATING

With the invention of the phonograph, all at once the great orchestras of the world became accessible everywhere. Despite a less-than-perfect sound quality, this novelty was an attraction for all the neighbours. The boy seems fascinated by the wax roll, which, a few moments earlier, allowed the strains of the beautiful *Blue Danube* to filter through the speaker. 1901.

△ MAIN STREET

Movie theatres, whether in Gaspé or New York, always have a bright façade decorated with strings of flashing electric lights of every colour. The bank façades, in stark contrast, are severe and dark, protected by metal grillwork. But both held a prominent place on the main street of Bedford, Missisquoi. 1951.

△ CHAMBER MUSIC
In the era before high-fidelity recordings, the best way to hear music was from a live orchestra. From time to time, people came together in private homes to listen to a magical moment, a concert given by young and talented musicians. 1913.

▷ THE DOG'S REEL
With a satisfied smile, this habitant from the Île aux Grues plays a bit of fiddle music for his dog during a midday break.

◁ LIMESTONE

Montreal buildings were predominantly made of grey limestone, commonly
known as Montreal greystone. A civic ordnance of 1721 made the stone mandatory
for house construction after a fire destroyed many of the city's buildings. Victorian
architects often succeeded in making the dull grey colour come alive with Gothic
detailing. 1910.

△ MOTHERS AND DAUGHTERS

It is always moving, even today, when four generations of the same family and
of the same gender are gathered together. At a time when life expectancy was
about 60, this was quite an achievement. The grandmother sits enthroned in her
richly carved armchair, each representative of the next generation sits on a less
comfortable chair than that of the previous one. It is impossible to make a mistake:
the features, expressions, everything indicates that these women are related. 1930.

△ THE TOWERS
The towers of the Sulpician farm are all that remain of its 17th century buildings. The turrets originally had a defensive role, protecting the occupants from attack. By the early 19th century they were merely decorative. An observer wrote about the gardens in 1839: "They are in summer the weekly resort of professors and pupils of the Seminary and College; and nothing can be better adapted for exercise, and recreation from sedentary employment. They march to and from the place in regular order, and are generally accompanied by a band of music, formed from amateurs of their own body."

▷ THE PLEASURE GARDEN
Thanks to a flourishing business, Isaiah Préfontaine earned his place among the members of the influential circle at the Chamber of Commerce and the Board of Trade in Montreal. Nonetheless, he maintained his ties to the city of his birth, Beloeil, where he built his summer home, villa des Épinettes. 1910.

◁ **LORD STRATHCONA**

The demolition of Lord Strathcona's house in the 1940s was a tragedy for Montreal's architectural heritage. Located on the present site of the Canadian Centre for Architecture, the Strathcona mansion bore the stamp of many architects, including this conservatory designed by Edward Maxwell. Lord Strathcona was born Donald Smith. He was associated with the Hudson's Bay Company for 72 years, rising from the position of clerk to the governorship. While a young fur trader, he built a garden in Rigolet on the Labrador coast, which brought accolades from surprised arctic explorers.

△ **LE CHÂTEAU**

After his country house burned down in 1896, Louis-Joseph Forget commissioned the rising star of Montreal architecture, Edward Maxwell, to design an even grander residence in the château style. The style was popular with the Canadian Pacific Railway for their stations and hotels. Forget was the first French-Canadian appointed to the CPR's board of directors. Maxwell designed an impressive three-storey fieldstone château, decorated with corbels, towers and spires. The grounds were first laid out by the Olmstead Brothers, the renowned firm of landscape architects, and completed by Frederick Todd. 1901.

△ LES GROISARDIÈRES

On the island that is the cradle of Québec, it is surprising to find an Italian garden. Nestled among the centuries-old farms on Île d'Orlèans, the Porteous family built a garden on their summer estate, Les Groisardières. Their house and garden are among the few in Québec that exhibit strong European influences and pretensions. Elaborate stonework was used to retain flowerbeds on the sharply sloping property and to serve as pedestals for a collection of urns and statuary.

▷ LITTLE TEMPLE

The Hodgson family was one of the first to settle the slopes of the mountain overlooking Montreal. This pavilion, probably designed as a small house for the children, is a perfect example of Victorian exuberance and is the centre of attraction in the garden. 1881.

◁ **SAINT ANNE, PATRON SAINT OF SAILORS**
Long before the great fire of 1922, the church of Sainte-Anne-de-
Beaupré was impressive. Large and majestic, it contained magnificent
works prepared in gold by Ranvoyzé and Amyot and sculptures made by
Levasseur and F. Baillairgé. These objects, saved from the fire, inspired
reconstruction of the church when it was decided to offer Saint Anne,
patron saint of sailors, a monumental temple whose splendour and
beauty would be unequalled in North America. c. 1910.

△ **UNDER THE SHEEPSKIN**
Once the snow has melted for good and the roads are dry, it will be
possible to bring out the wheeled vehicles. In the interim, the sleigh,
capable of travelling over snow as well as frozen ground, is still
necessary. 1911.

◁ LE CHÂTEAU DES FÉES

The Hodgson family discovered the Laurentians at the turn of the century. Made accessible by the extension of the railway in 1892, Montrealers acquired properties on the lakes near Sainte-Agathe-des-Monts. Thomas Hodgson built a log house on Lac Brulé. The house was among several log buildings designed by architect Edward Maxwell. Not only was the house built of logs, but the veranda that surrounded the house on three sides was supported by tree trunks, adding to the rusticity of the building. The house was decorated with flowerbeds, bringing charm to a bucolic setting. 1910.

△ THE BRIDGE

The little wooden bridge, the girls, their slightly melancholy gaze directed downwards – all these details recall that this kind of staging was aimed at achieving a certain aestheticism. Only the dog did not understand the photographer's instructions. c. 1910.

A GOOD SPOT

A wealthy hotel promoter once said that only one criterion determines commercial success: location. This wise principle was probably followed by the owner of the Boucherie Pelletier. A good spot, located at the corner of two of the most heavily travelled streets, ensures that people will notice. But this is not enough. An arabesque-covered pediment and three large signs, one depicting healthy cattle, catches the eye: this is definitely the butcher's shop. c. 1910.

THE PHARMACY

Potions, remedies, syrups, all were sold by the pharmacist. The layout, cleanliness and orderliness of the premises in Rivière-du-Loup reflect the seriousness, trust and integrity of the business and of those who work there. The large counters allow the staff, all dressed in black, to serve the customer in complete privacy. The presence of religious statues indicates that, with God's help, everyone will soon be better. c. 1910.

△ WHOLESALE DELIVERY

Soap, jams, sacks of grain, and potatoes were just a few of the things distributed by the wholesaler L.H. Levasseur. Their pride evident on their faces, these deliverymen were happy to abandon the horse-drawn wagon for the more efficient truck. Not only could it carry five times the amount of goods, but the comfort and conveniences were also impressive: wooden wheels surrounded by rubber, a tarp to protect the occupants from bad weather and a windshield. 1925.

▷ SUMMER IN SAINTE-ANNE-DE-BEAUPRÉ

To celebrate the feast day of Saint Anne, people came from far and wide, using all means of transportation – car, train, boat or even on foot – to return home with a rosary, a pennant or a medal.

SNOW DEPOTS

When the St. Lawrence River was too far away, the carters designated
a hill, an embankment or a slope to dump the snow collected from
the streets. This photo shows the Belvédère Hill in Quebec City, located
above the industrial area seen in the background.

HOUSE CALLS

Since he might be called out to visit the sick at any time, Doctor Kane quickly purchased the latest invention: the automobile. Even snow-covered roads could not prevent him from fulfilling his duty, thanks to the chains on the tires, the lanterns located on each side of the car and the recycled cover from an old sleigh. 1911.

FRESH VEGETABLES

It is difficult to find a more animated scene than this public market in August 1942. Women and men, young and old, try to clear a path between the stalls where large, wicker bushels of apples, baskets of tomatoes, bags of potatoes and stacks of empty crates are standing. Some markets were held in halls, but the farmers and customers visiting the Saint-Roch market in Quebec City have nothing but black cloths stretched out over their stalls or their own hat for protection against the sun's scorching rays.

◁ VIEUX SÉMINAIRE

The garden of the Vieux Séminaire in the heart of Old Montreal is the birthplace of gardening in North America. Seigneurs of Montreal from 1663, the Sulpicians built a seminary on Rue Notre-Dame in 1685. Maps show many gardens within the city walls. At the Vieux Séminaire, the gardens were a series of formal parterres arranged around a central fountain or statue. Over time this sacred space has been reduced in size. Although the gardens were among the first in Canada to be designated of national historic significance, they still await restoration. 1870.

△ ON THE ROAD

Motorized vehicles, with their superior speed and endurance, quickly replaced the horse for the transport of goods and passengers over long distances. Gleaming buses, capable of carrying up to 10 passengers, began criss-crossing the roads and opening the way for regular intercity public transit. c. 1920.

△ THE PRISON FOR WOMEN

The Maison Gomin was built in the early 1930s in Sainte-Foy to house prisoners. Eventually reserved for female prisoners, the building, which is now completely surrounded by grass, continues to make its own particular mark on the built-up landscape around it.

FIRE!

▷ In January 1926, a major fire struck one of the most prestigious buildings in the capital. Fortunately, the firemen succeeded in containing the damage to one section of the building. This photograph shows the limited resources available to the firemen. Around the same time, several famous, historic buildings that reflected Québec's architectural heritage went up in flames due to the lack of effective fire protection.

THE GREAT FIRE

The Great Fire of Hull burned everything in its path, including these railway cars that were once laden with wood. The fire broke out around 10 a.m. on April 26, 1900, in a chimney on St. Redempteur Street in Hull. By midnight, the fire had consumed more than 3,000 buildings and left 15,000 without homes. It caused over $10 million in damage. Half of Hull and one fifth of Ottawa were razed. The sawmills in both cities were entirely destroyed by the flames. With the Parliament buildings in the background, the smouldering remains are a stark reminder of the day's events.

TRICENTENARY

Celebrating Quebec City's tricentenary, rue Saint-Jean is bustling in 1908. Soldiers are marching before a crowd assembled at windows and on the sidewalks. Some of us still remember the most famous street in Quebec City, when the awnings, polished cobblestones, tramways and famous shops livened up the capital.

△ SUNDAY ONLOOKERS

During the war, the curious had a lot to look at; not a week went by during which destroyers, frigates, torpedo boats and other allied ships did not call at the Port of Quebec City. Some of them carried important people, heads of state or high-ranking army officers who were participating in conferences and strategic meetings.

▷ WAR HERO

The First World War brought grief to each town and village in the country. Too often, a funeral procession would pass with soldiers carrying a coffin draped with the British flag. On this day in 1915, the funeral services of Private Therrien serve as a reminder to Rivière-du-Loup of the slaughter going on in Europe.

190

◁ RUE RACINE, CHICOUTIMI

On this commercial street, the seamstress, lingerie seller, watchmaker, launderer, barber, grocer and billiard hall are found side by side. The rise in elevation in the middle of the road allowed for rainwater to drain along the edge of the sidewalks, as there was no storm sewer system yet. Three modes of transportation are seen here: the bicycle, the automobile and the horse. c. 1915.

△ THE TOBACCO HARVEST

As the summer progressed, rows of tobacco leaves would be broken to allow them to dry in the sun, until they were harvested. Once fall arrived, only the smallest, thinnest leaves at the top remained on the stems and were left on the fields in Saint-Henri-de-Taillon, Lac-Saint-Jean.

◁ **THE RIVER CROSSING FOR HORSES**

No boats could navigate the rapids of the St. Maurice River, and the water was much too cold to walk through. Hanging in mid-air, blindfolded, the horse remains still while being transported across the river. Supplies destined for the logging camps took the same route.

△ **"TWENTY-FIVE MILE FLIGHT. THE SURPRISE OF YOUR LIFE"**

In the summer of 1930, brothers Arthur and Joseph Fecteau from Sainte-Marie-de-Beauce criss-crossed the province offering people the chance to try flying for the first time. One day, just to spice things up, Arthur jumped from a height of 915 metres above the St. Lawrence using a patched-up parachute from the First World War. By 1960, Arthur owned 25 airplanes to serve the Saguenay, Lac-Saint-Jean and Abitibi regions, and all of northwestern Québec. 1957.

△ UNDER THE CANVAS

Every traveller packed a tent. The forest provided the poles to hold it up. This portable shelter, easy to assemble and disassemble, proved indispensable during rainy evenings. On a clear and starry night, an upside down canoe also did the trick.

▷ THE VILLA MENIER

Anticosti Island sits at the mouth of the St. Lawrence. In 1895, this huge forested area became the property of a wealthy French chocolate manufacturer, Henri Menier. A few years later, he ordered the construction of a splendid villa based on the drawings of the Parisian architect Sauvestre. Menier held memorable receptions to which he invited illustrious guests. 1906.

A SUPPLY OF CONES

Sometimes, the forest needs a helping hand to regenerate. Since 1908, the employees of the Centre des sémences forestières de Berthier have been climbing ladders or using a pole to collect softwood cones. These are dried, then stored. An expert ensures that they are neither deformed nor damaged by insects. With these seeds, the nursery grower will be able to grow seedlings to reforest those areas that have difficulty regenerating naturally.

MIDNIGHT MASS

On Christmas Eve at the Dallaire camp, the priest took advantage of the clerk's sleigh to head up to the camp to hear confession. Thus, the men could receive communion during midnight mass. Then the men would push the tables into a corner and the loggers would dance a "square set" while trying not to think about family gatherings back home.

△ TIME TO DO THE DISHES

After eating dinner prepared over the campfire, these men would do the dishes. Smoking a pipe to keep the bugs away, the three divide the task: Gagné will wash, Leblanc will dry and Simard will store the kit in a large linen sack. Before leaving, the men will generously douse the fire to put it out. 1913.

▷ BIRCHBARK

George Mattaway and his family found everything they needed to make their wigwams on the banks of the Camatose River in the Ottawa Valley. They needed tree trunks to make the conical frame and birch bark to cover it. In one hour, the Algonquins could build themselves a home. Even in the 1940s, birchbark remained indispensable to Aboriginal peoples, who used it to produce all kinds of containers, boxes, baskets, plates, portage sacks and canoes. 1940.

◁ THE PULLMAN CAR

Many railway cars were built by the Pullman Palace-Car Company in Pullman, Illinois. They took their name from the car's inventor, George Pullman. He is credited with perfecting rail cars, making them both comfortable and clean, and which allowed for the rapid conversion of coaches into sleeping cars. In 1865, he patented the first Pullman sleeping car; it allowed the coach seat to fold down into a bed and the upper berth to descend from hinges on the car's ceiling. Here a group of distinguished visitors emerge from the comfortable confines of their Pullman car in Montreal, 1897.

△ RADIO

The Canadian National was the first railway in the world to add a radio car to its trains. Individual headphones were added to the library car. Passengers could tune into one of 10 broadcasting stations CN had established. A wireless operator ensured that the signal came in loud and clear. The CN wireless system was the precursor to Canada's transcontinental broadcasting system.

△ THE NEW BRIDGE

In July 1836, wooden tracks covered with iron rails linked La Prairie to Saint-Jean-sur-Richelieu. This track was 10 inches wider than the type used in the United States to prevent the Americans from using the railroad to invade Canada. In 1850, the rail network in Québec was less than seventy miles long.

▷ JUNCTION

This is the junction of the street railways at the corner of St. Catherine and St. Laurent in 1893. The construction of the street railways caused massive dislocation in the urban environment. Both in Montreal and Quebec City, the arrival of the street railways led to the loss of trees, the widening of streets and changes to the intimacy of many squares and civic spaces.

◁ **CONSTANT IMPROVEMENT**

The history of railways since the 1920s has essentially been one of improving the efficiency of the existing network. Almost no track has been added. Rather, railway companies have concentrated on increasing traffic and profits on their existing infrastructure. One of the ways of doing so was to increase the tonnage transported by using larger cars and longer trains. The larger cars required heavier engines and sometimes also demanded improvements to ties, bridges and culverts. The wheels, and particularly the axles, had to bear the increased burden. 1946.

△ **BANANAS**

With the coming of refrigerated rail cars, fruits, vegetables, meat and dairy produce could all be transported quickly and safely over long distances. Bananas, previously a very rare and expensive treat, were sent from the West Indies all across Canada, tens-of-thousands at a time.

DOCUMENTARY ART

Some photographs so transcend time that they cease to be documentary and become art. This photograph, taken by William Notman in May 1859, shows engine number 209, "Trevithick." Set against the background of the Grand Trunk Railway shop in Point St. Charles, the photograph illustrates the pride of the men associated with the railway.

THE ROUNDHOUSE

The purpose of the roundhouse was to make it possible to turn the locomotives around quickly for servicing. Crews worked round-the-clock and employees were on call to conduct emergency work. The locomotive was the powerhouse of the railway. As such, an out-of-service locomotive was lost money. The roundhouse was organized much like a pit stop; the foreman's task was to return the locomotive to active service as quickly as possible.

◁ **WEAVING MILL**

Linen production had long remained a craft. However, by 1950 the weaving mill in Plessisville was at the technological forefront. The complex machinery accomplished the tasks that had traditionally been carried out in a family context using rudimentary tools. The ingenuity of the men who developed and assembled these steel giants can only be admired, all the more so since these machines were built on site at the Plessisville foundry. 1950

△ **DIRIGIBLE**

During the 1920s aircraft technology evolved making it possible to transport hundreds of passengers at one time over the Atlantic. The R-100, an enormous dirigible stretching 225 metres, flew over the St. Lawrence River Valley in late July 1930. In this photo, it is anchored to its mooring mast at Saint-Hubert Airport, the largest in the country at the time.

MILKMAN

Countrymen are often creative and good with their hands. This man in Sainte-Félicité, Matane, used the undercarriage of an old car to build a milk delivery wagon. The result is a unique and practical vehicle, which must have given the milkman pleasure every day on his route.

AN EARLY SNOWMOBILE

In areas like Témiscouata, Rimouski, the Gaspé Peninsula, the North Shore and the Saguenay, the snowmobile maintained the link between the countryside and the town during the long winter. 1949.

212

◁ THE GARAGE

The blacksmith, harness maker and saddler had to quickly reinvent themselves; a new era had begun, that of the car. The reassuring company of teams of horses and quiet streets would, in no time, be replaced by an increasing number of fast cars spitting out noise and carbon monoxide. The first garages were, for most people, a curiosity where one could observe the unending gymnastics of the mechanics without really understanding what they were doing. c. 1918.

△ THE MOTORCYCLIST

With goggles and gloves, this early motorcyclist is set to experience travelling at a speed unheard of just a few years earlier.

COVERED BRIDGE

Covered bridges like this
one on the Cascapédia River,
Bonaventure protected
travellers in horse-drawn
carriages from storms and
rain. They also became a
meeting place for young
people who hid inside to scare
the horses and sometimes the
people who crossed them on
foot. In some places, the town
had to post a guard.

214

◁ SEIGNEURIAL SYSTEM

In New France, the lands along the St. Lawrence were divided into rectangles and granted to seigneurs. The seigneurs then divided the grants into tenure lots that were offered to the first settlers and their descendants for a fee. After 1760, the new British government undertook the division of available land into townships where the lots were free of any fees. Thus, vast, square parcels of land opened up to settlement in the Eastern Townships, then inland from the seigneuries located on the Laurentian plain. This aerial photo shows the Lessard and Rimouski seigneuries next to the river's edge and the divided townships located inland. The seigneurial system was not abolished until 1854.

△ OPEN COCKPIT

In the early 1930s, both pilot and passenger in a single-engine aircraft sat in an open cockpit. To protect themselves against the cold and wind, they wore goggles, a leather cap, jacket, boots and gloves all made of leather. In winter, they had to add a leather facemask.

LIGHTHOUSE

Located opposite Saint-Jean-Port-Joli, the Rocher Algernon lighthouse was built in 1870 on a rock that was covered by water at half tide. A keeper occupied the lighthouse until 1927. The spirit of sacrifice of the keepers who existed in these kinds of living conditions was such that their only request was to live on solid ground during the winter months.

△ PILOT'S ROWBOAT

Since the beginning of settlement, pilots in their rowboats would approach large vessels that were underway to offer their services. Each spring, the pilots waited with their rowboats for the arrival of the great sailing ships or steamships in order to take them to Quebec City. Once the pilot had taken charge of the ship, the trip from Bic to Quebec City would take eight days, while the return would take only five. In rough weather on the return trip, faced with the impossibility of disembarking, several pilots had to continue on to England and return on the next ship. c. 1890.

▷ A FOREST OF MASTS

During the summer months, there were so many ships in the port of Quebec City that the towering masts with their yards made both sides of the river look like a forest of dried trees. The discipline observed while on board the sailing ships during the crossing prompted crews to unwind during port visits when it became possible to leave the ship. c. 1860.

THE PORT OF MONTREAL

In the 19th century, the Port of Montreal was an ongoing construction site whose appearance changed constantly. Thanks to steam travel, dragging of the river and construction of the canals linking the Great Lakes, the city succeeded in replacing Quebec City as the main port of entry to the St. Lawrence by the end of the century. 1878.

SMALL BOATS

During summer, the loading, repair and supply of the boats anchored at Quebec City required a lot of manpower and the services of all types of workers, merchants and agents. Everything travelled by water, with each group owning its own boat. The ships' suppliers used sturdy boats such as these to supply the ships. c. 1905.

△ **IMMIGRANTS ARRIVING AT THE PORT OF QUEBEC CITY**
At the beginning of the 20th century, more than a million immigrants left their homeland each year for North America seeking their fortune. At that time, an ocean crossing was not a pleasant outing, but a long and uncertain adventure during which the dangers of sea travel were always present in the mind of the traveller. 1911.

▷ **PASTIMES ON BOARD THE *EMPRESS OF BRITAIN***
During the crossing to Canada, many evenings ended with the playing of joyous music. Some danced a jig while others danced folkdances to the sounds of the fiddle. 1910.

◁ THE SS *ROYAL GEORGE*

On November 6, 1912, during its last voyage of the season, the Canadian Northern Railway's passenger liner *Royal George* ran aground downstream from the St. Lawrence dock on the Île d'Orléans. The ship was refloated and temporarily repaired in Quebec City after having suffered serious damage. Fearing that it would be caught in ice over the winter, the ship quickly left for Halifax on December 12. Since the channel buoys had already been removed for the winter, the ship was escorted by the lighthouse tender *Montmagny* until it reached the ferry crossing at Saint-Roch located further downriver.

△ GIANTS OF THE SEA

View of the stern of the *Montrose*, a 16,401-tonne passenger liner. Of all things man-made, maritime shipping, without a doubt, best demonstrates the gigantic proportions that are possible. The liners, which were the heirs of the great sailing ships, represent the culmination of a series of technological innovations that magnified the propulsion, speed and tonnage of ships.

THE SECOND LIGHTHOUSE AT MATANE IN 1906
Entering service in 1873, the Matane lighthouse was part of a small structure that also served as the keeper's home. During the early years, the keepers complained of its small size and isolation. The first keeper was even forced to move into another home in Matane in the winter of 1877 because of the cold. Constructed too close to the sea and exposed to the erosion of the cliff, the lighthouse was moved back 100 feet in 1884.

THE ÎLET ROUGE LIGHTHOUSE

Built in 1848, the Îlet Rouge lighthouse was situated on a vast area of dangerous shoals lying in the middle of the St. Lawrence near the mouth of the Saguenay. Several round towers, such as the one at Îlet Rouge, served as lodgings for the keepers and their families, in spite of the intense cold and constant humidity that prevailed in these stone towers.

GOOD CATCH

Filling a boat with cod using a jig to catch the fish can easily exhaust
a man. Alone, standing in the boat with a line in each hand, the
fisherman would spend the day balancing on one foot, then the other
in order to jiggle the fish hook dropped over each side of the boat. 1941.

CLEANING THE CATCH

A table for cleaning cod was placed on the shore in L'Anse-aux-Gascons to fillet the fish and remove the head and dorsal fin. The waste was tossed back into the sea and the meat moved in carts to the fish flakes where it could dry in the sun.

231

DRESSING COD

In Gaspé, teenage boys and young men were often employed in the fish processing plants to dress, fillet and package the cod sent to markets throughout North America.

A 60-POUND COD

In Percé in the early 1950s, it was not unusual to catch large cod. There was no talk at the time of overfishing. Today, it is completely different. As Mr. Noël, an old seahound living in Anse-à-la-Barbe, pointed out, "Today, a fisherman would go all the way to Quebec City to have his picture taken if he caught a 100-pound cod."

TROUT FISHERMEN
The guide and packers accompany the trout fishermen to the camp on Lake Rossignol. First, they had to cross several kilometres of forest.

DIFFERENT TIME, DIFFERENT CUSTOMS

During May, 1929, teams of men worked on the carcasses of approximately 50 beluga whales lying on a beach, trying to remove the valuable fat before the next tide took away the dead animals. Belugas were fished commercially in the St. Lawrence until the 1950s.

◁ **PORTAGE**

His load on his back and tumpline around his forehead, Sylvestre Kapu rests for a moment. He is carrying a 120-pound sack of beans, two buckets of fat each weighing 50 pounds and another sack on top. However, this is not his first portage; he knows how to distribute his load and how to place his foot on the path before transferring his weight.

△ **THE RAPIDS**

At the foot of the Iroquois Rapids on the Vermillon River, the canoeist can portage by pulling the canoe using a cord slung over the shoulder or can flip the canoe onto the shoulders or grip the canoe on one side and move it around the rocks and through the turbulent water.

WINTER CAMP

The Montagnais lived in close harmony with nature and moved according to the seasons. At the end of summer, the family of Johnny Piastitute packed up and left the banks of the river in birch bark canoes to head out to the winter hunting grounds. The canoe was placed on a sled and the snowshoes would soon be needed to move over the snow.

AMONG THE MONTAGNAIS OF POINTE-BLEUE
Among most of the aboriginal peoples, it was the women who were
responsible for preparing skins and producing clothing, shoes and
snowshoes. It was an art to make the webbing of the snowshoe so
delicately and consistently.

LES ESCOUMINS

A trip along the north shore of the St. Lawrence River would not be complete without a stop at one of the aboriginal villages scattered along the shore. Here, about 1913, the Ross family proudly welcomes visitors to the point at Les Escoumins. It was an opportunity to buy woven baskets, nicely decorated moccasins and other examples of Montagnais crafts.

243

THE WINDS

Faced with the constant, strong winds, some islanders on Île-aux-Coudres constructed low-rise, square, stone houses with the main floor situated just above the ground. The low attic, simple roof and narrow openings vaguely recall the thatched cottages of Ireland or Scotland, which face the same conditions. There, as here, little is left for the wind to take, the precious warmth of the hearth or the stove is not wasted heating empty space.

244

A GOOD PIPE

This couple is waiting their turn to mill grain in Morel de Val-Jalbert in the Lac-Saint-Jean area around 1925. The wait would depend more or less on how much water entered the sluiceway to turn the millstones, but a good pipe of Canadian tobacco helped to pass the time.

MAKING CHARCOAL

Hardwood waste was continuously heated in these furnaces surrounded by white snow. Businessman Alexandre Paquet owned about twenty such wood charcoal furnaces. From 1939 to 1945, demand for wood charcoal was very strong for use in the production of explosives. After the war, Mr. Paquet sold his operations to the steel mills. 1948.

DOUBLE SHIFT

The farmer knew, from birth, what life held in store for him. In summer,
he cleared, ploughed, planted and harvested; in winter, he headed off
to the forest, where the tough life of the logger awaited him. The axe,
hand saw and two-handed saw replaced the harrow and scythe. c. 1900.

△ GLEANING THE LOGS

Once the big logs had passed, men headed out in canoes to gather the logs that had run aground on the river banks or ended up in still water on the Batiscan River. The collected logs were bound together using pins to form a raft that would become increasingly impressive as it travelled down the river. This rudimentary raft, steered using a pike pole, carried the canoe. Performed each year, this work always took a few weeks. 1942.

▷ LOGJAM

Pike pole and log turner in hand, the drivers constantly braved the cold, snow and water. With hobnailed boots on their feet, they ran over the logs that continually moved. If, unfortunately, a man fell into the water, his heavy clothes would inexorably draw him down to the bottom. It is easy to understand why most drivers were bachelors.

SETTLEMENT

During the Depression of the 1930s, the families of many unemployed men lived in misery. Abbé Jean, of the Société de la colonisation de Sainte-Anne-de-la-Pocatière, recruited families from Kamouraska and L'Islet counties and helped them settle in Roquemaure, Abitibi. The settlers were given food and everything they needed to get through their first winter, but the work was very hard. They had to build a cabin, clear the land, and prepare the soil for planting seeds among the stumps. 1934.

VISITORS

Special excursions were organized for aspiring settlers in the 1930s. Accompanied by a missionary priest, they visited the new parishes and met the land agent as well as established settlers. Some took advantage of the trip to visit relatives. Abbé Maurice Proulx, who was passing through Sainte-Anne-de-Roquemaure during filming of his documentary, *En pays neufs* ("In New Lands"), photographed these visitors who posed in front of the family's first log cabin, which had been converted to a stable. 1935.

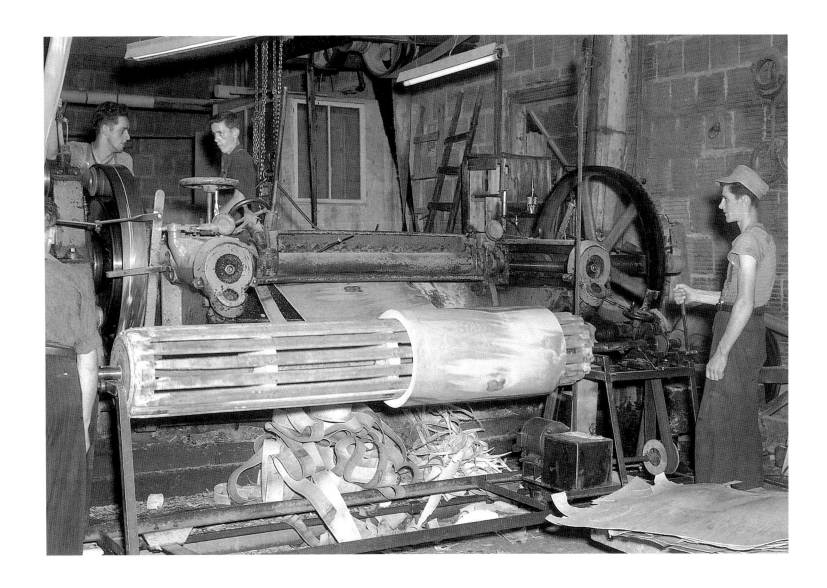

◁ BARREL STAVES

Barrels, used for storing everything from apples, molasses, flour, lard and fish to rum, gas and nails, were all made from staves. They rolled easily and could be stacked in a ship's hold, a carter's cart or a merchant's cellar. When the Basques came to hunt whale off Trois-Pistoles, they brought staves with them to assemble as needed to store melted whale fat.

△ SHEETS OF WOOD

Employees at Placo Ltd. in Tring-Jonction unwind a beautiful hardwood log, previously stripped of its bark. A large, steel knife penetrates the soaked log while it is turning and peels it in one continuous motion. A thin sheet of wood begins to extend little by little. It will be used to make small fruit baskets and bushels for apples. However, the most beautiful pieces will be saved for producing plywood. 1950.

△ THE LITTLE MATCH LOCOMOTIVE

Ezra Butler Eddy, "King of the Match", born in the U.S. but a Québecker by adoption, was an important industrialist in Hull. His enterprising spirit also made him one of the first lumber barons to produce wood pulp, an essential ingredient in the making of paper. The E .B. Eddy Manufacturing Company had its own train, nicknamed "Nettie."

▷ THE SAWMILL

Sawmill employees worked for hours at a time at a fast pace. Standing on the carriage, they had to continuously position and reposition the logs before locking them into place using a log dog. The grinding of the saws was deafening, as was the noise of the slabs, planks and boards falling on to the conveyor. 1944.

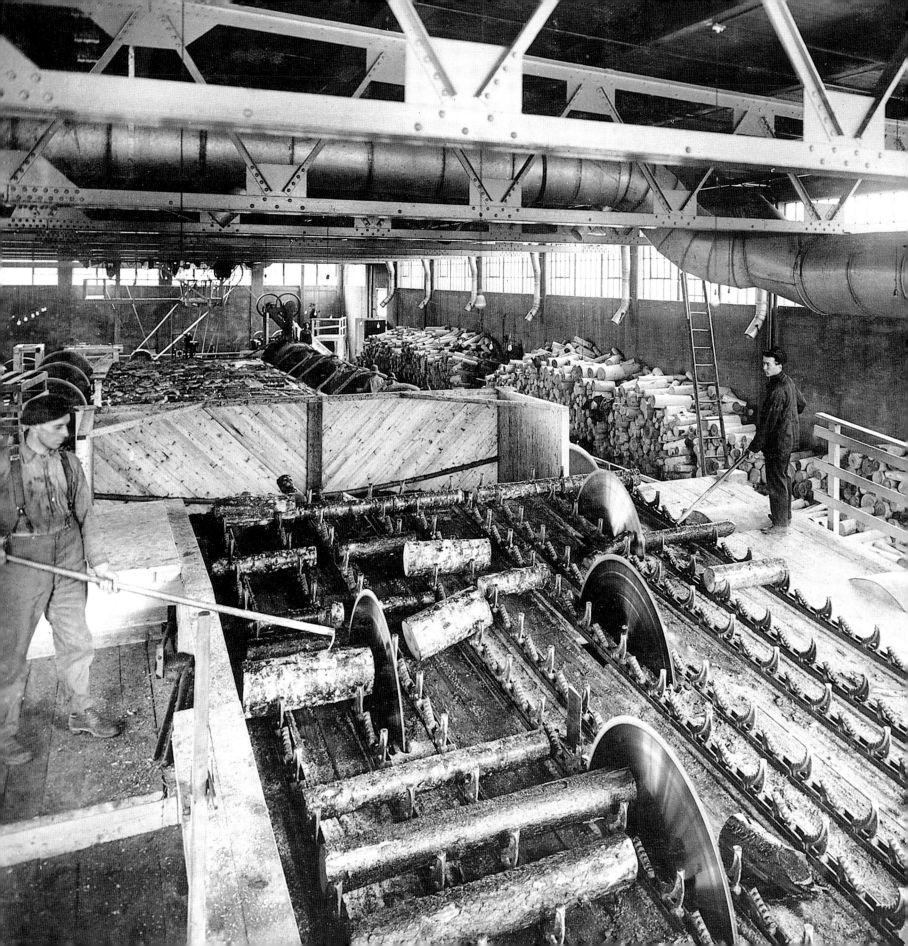

◁ CROSS-CUTTING

The conveyor drops the logs onto a big, inclined ramp that occupies a large part of the St. Lawrence Pulp and Lumber Corporation mill. A series of circular saws placed at regular intervals cut the wood into saw-ends of 12, 8, 4 and 2 feet. Men posted on each side observe this dangerous operation.

△ ARRIVAL OF THE RAFTS

On the banks of the St. Lawrence near Quebec City, men disassemble the wooden rafts that the raftsmen have brought down from the Great Lakes and the Ottawa Valley. These huge platforms, made from square timber bound together and covered with planks, were steered by teams of 20 to 30 men. The drivers would set up their tents or build simple shelters on their floating rafts, and the cook would make a fire in a large tub filled with sand to prepare the meals. c. 1875.

WOOD AND IMMIGRANTS

Ships built in Quebec City were sold primarily to English shipowners. They sailed to England loaded with wood and returned to Canada filled with immigrants and a variety of goods. The fastest ships, the ones that drew attention to themselves during the ocean crossing, were sent around the world on behalf of their new owners. In 1870, these three-masters averaged between 18 and 22 days to cross the Atlantic. 1872.

THE PORT OF QUEBEC CITY

In 1860, at the time of the timber trade, it was easy to recognize the old sailing ships by the fake portholes painted on their bulwark. In the past, these openings were made in the side of the hull to allow for cannon muzzles to pass through. At the beginning of the 19th century, merchant ships, still fearing acts of piracy on the Atlantic, were disguised using this trick, which, from a distance, gave the appearance of cannons on board, thereby discouraging any potential attackers.

259

△ WOOD FOR SHIPS

The free entry of Canadian wood into England spurred shipbuilding in the 19th century. In Quebec City, many ships, hastily built to earn money, were sold at a considerable profit after only a few voyages. Some ships were even constructed using square timber to be disassembled and sold for wood once they arrived at their destination. 1872.

▷ LOADING WOOD

Labouring under the hot summer sun, the stowers used a winch and tackle to load the square timber. The availability of a cargo door near the stem, almost at water level, made it easier to load long pieces of wood into the ship's hold. This square opening would then be permanently sealed with a solid, caulked panel before the ship set sail.

△ STEAM POWER

In 1842, steamships began travelling from the port of Quebec City to the Saguenay River. During the trip, the ships had to make several stops, not only to take on passengers but also to refuel. They stopped at La Malbaie and Rivière-du-Loup, then the cove at Eau at the mouth of the majestic Saguenay. Once the steamship had docked, the firewood stacked on the docks was loaded. These cruise ships took their passengers all the way to Chicoutimi. c. 1890.

▷ THE FLOATING DOCK

Before the invention of the dry dock, grounding ships between tides was the only way to repair or maintain the hull. However, beginning in 1827, ingenious Québec shipbuilders succeeded in perfecting the floating dock. They were the first in North America to develop this technique for lifting boats. Until 1878, nine floating docks were in use in Québec shipyards. These enormous, well-built boxes were capable of accommodating ships measuring up to 190 feet.

PREPARING FOR WINTER

When the men were away hunting, the Montagnais women took care of the camp set up near the Toulnustouc River. As winter approached, the women would prepare the reserves of firewood. Equipped with a handsaw, young Sophie Benoît does her part. 1939.

BEAST OF BURDEN

The eyes of the ox are half closed, its muzzle covered with slobber, its neck straining with the effort. In the settlement areas and the vast forests of Abitibi, this animal was highly appreciated, not only for its strength, but also for the minimal care it required. The settlers yoked it to uproot trees, remove large logs from the forest and plough their land.

△ CUTTING WOOD

Small businessmen who exploited the vast forests of the Saguenay region moved into small houses attached to the stable, sometimes with their families, sometimes with their brothers, cousins and a few hired hands. An exhausting job lay ahead, for in the spring, they had to deliver 250 cords of wood. The loggers felled and debranched the trees, carted off the logs and stacked them. The women prepared the meals, did the laundry and kept the books. The children harnessed their dogs to a sled and brought supplies to the men.

▷ READY FOR WINTER

In Saint-Raphaël-de-Bellechasse, the entire Gagnon family came together behind the barn to prepare the firewood. The gas engine was brought out from the shed and the large splitter belt attached. This was assembly-line work. Perched on top of the pile, the mother drops the billets towards the two youngest children, who then give them to the older ones. They, in turn, pass them to their father, who places them in the splitter to split them into quarters. About 15 cords of wood were kept for the house; the rest could be sold in the village. 1944.

SURVEYING THE LINE

Railway building involves three stages: the location of the line, clearing the right of way and construction itself. Surveying the line was often the most difficult part. The survey crews cleared a line with axes and saws. Using a rod and telescope and taking bearings from the sun's position, the chief surveyor mapped the terrain and established the eventual route. The work was hard, hot and often buggy. Here, a survey crew of the Intercolonial Railway poses with their equipment in the summer of 1869.

△ THE FLUME INSPECTOR

Millions of gallons of water transported thousands of cords of wood in Gatineau. The sluice gate of the dam feeding the flume is closed. A man is surveying the long ribbon of wood to check the condition of the walls. Now is the time to replace rotting boards, to seal the cracks and to raise the sections that have sagged. c. 1880.

▷ THE LAURENTIAN FLUME

Sometimes logs were sent one at a time down a water-filled flume that encircled hills and spanned valleys and rivers for kilometres. Built on wooden trestles, these flumes were constructed in areas where floating the logs down a river was either very difficult or impossible. Whatever the weather, men walked the wooden walkway alongside the flume to watch the logs come down. Simple shelters were built at a few strategic points to allow the men to stay dry.

TEMPORARY CAMP

In 1913, during the preliminary work on the Gouin Dam, the company responsible for the work set up temporary camps to house the workers. The men chose a suitable site to pitch the tents, then cleared it using the fir tree trunks as frames. Lefebvre, Beausoleil and Beaudry had to carry out the exploratory work. They are shown here in front of their office.

RUNNING WATER

The population growth experienced in Québec starting in the 1850s created a need for more drinking water. Before pipes and water distribution systems could be built, artificial lakes had to be created using dikes and dams. Completely made of wood, this type of dam, circa 1910, was common throughout Québec. Although easy and economical to build, it had a short life span and was difficult to maintain.

◁ THE VIADUCT

The Cap Rouge viaduct, west of Quebec City, is one of the most remarkable engineering works in Canada. It was built between 1906 and 1912 and is known locally as "Le Tracel," derived from the English word "trestle," the term used to describe these monumental viaducts, more often made of wood than steel. c. 1916.

△ THE DRYING YARD

In the late 19th century, labourers used carts to move planks to the drying yard of the sawmills located at the foot of the Montmorency Falls. To make the job easier, a passageway was covered with wooden planks. In the yard, pilers climbed onto the planks to build higher and higher wooden cages. c. 1880.

△ THE SWING BRIDGE

The swing bridge was one of the more complicated railway structures. It rotated to let ships pass. The swing bridge on Montreal's Lachine Canal required piers to be built in the middle of the canal. It was not popular with ship captains who had to navigate around this unnatural obstacle. Out of use for decades, a swing bridge on the Lachine Canal survives, a vestige of the era when railways and canals both flourished. 1901.

▷ LOG SLIDES

During the winter, it was possible to transport logs by sending them down a long timber chute. With a bit of shovelling to remove the snow, some pails of water to improve the ice here and there and a series of tripods to cross the swale, everything was ready for the logs to come flying down. During the winter of 1944/45, workers at the John Murdoch logging camp in Saint-Raymond constructed this chute to avoid having to haul the wood to the river.

THE MAIL CAR

Initially the train, which ran along the St. Lawrence, carried goods that had arrived in Quebec City or Montreal by ship. Trains were also used to carry passengers and to deliver the mail.

DERAILED

When this train derailed at Craigs Road on the main line of the Grand Trunk in the Chaudière-Appalaches region, crews and crowds rushed to the scene. Clearing the debris was the first step in what was inevitably a lengthy clean-up operation. An accident often led to a railway board of inquiry, and sometimes to a coroner's inquest. 1895.

◁ DISASTER

The train accident in Beloil on June 29, 1864, was the greatest railway disaster in Canadian history. One hundred passengers lost their lives when this train careened off the St. Hilaire bridge on the St. Lawrence and Atlantic Railroad. The accident was caused by a signalman's confusion. He was unaware that the swing bridge over the Richelieu River was open to let a steamer pass—and plunged the train into the river.

△ DEVASTATING POWER

A violent summer storm flooded the river and knocked out the bridge, leaving the track suspended in mid-air. 1917.

THE BRIDGE AT GRAND-MÉTIS

Even today, the work of the masons who built the stone piers on the Intercolonial is a marvel to behold. Large stones, weighing several tons each, were hoisted into place using the most elementary principles of mechanics. The substantial stone piers and steel viaducts seemed unnecessary to critics of the railway. They clamoured in Parliament for cheaper wooden trestles as news of the rising railway cost became public. Sandford Fleming stood fast, arguing that the initial investment was costly, but provided savings over the long term. The durability of the stonework is a testament to the builders. c. 1870.

TROIS-PISTOLES

The great clay cutting near Trois-Pistoles was a particularly difficult section for the Intercolonial Railway engineers and contractors. At the confluence of the Trois-Pistoles River and the St. Lawrence the hills were pure clay, too unstable to support the tracks. Removing this heavy, blue clay was a huge task. Only a spade could be used, as picks and shovels proved useless. The clay was cut into blocks and heaved into wagons using pitchforks. Even after the clay had been removed, the area was the site of several landslides because the exposed clay was unstable and became liquid after heavy rains. c. 1870.

283

◁ **DIVERTING THE RIVER**
   The Intercolonial Railway faced several challenges in laying the track.
   One of the greatest was the difficult section crossing the Tartigou River
   in eastern Québec. Here the path of the rail line left the highlands
   above the St. Lawrence and twisted south towards New Brunswick.
   To avoid building an expensive bridge over the river, they diverted the
   river by blasting a tunnel through the shale. c. 1870.

△ **THE STEAM SHOVEL**
   One piece of equipment that accelerated track laying was the steam
   shovel. It replaced countless labourers and their wheelbarrows. The
   steam shovel was transported to the railhead where it excavated
   material to be used as fill or ballast elsewhere. It was a great boon
   for railway contractors, for whom time was of the essence. Working
   under considerable pressure from the railway companies, their profits
   depended on their ability to complete the work on schedule and
   without cost overruns.

EARLY PHOTOGRAPHY

The tools of early photographers were both primitive and cumbersome. When Alexander Henderson photographed the construction of the Intercolonial, he set up a temporary darkroom along the line. In this photo, we catch a rare glimpse of his camera. The early cameras used what is called the "wet collodion process." The photographer had to travel with large glass plates that served as negatives. The plate was coated with an emulsion in a dark tent and then sensitized in a bath of silver nitrate. Once exposed in the camera, the plate was brought to the tent, where it was developed. c. 1879.

△ THE FLUME IN BEAUPRÉ

To get the timber to the mill, enormous flumes sometimes had to be built stretching over several miles. A continuous flow of water carried the logs along. However, as the forest retreated farther from the river, this way of moving logs was replaced by others, namely railroads and trucks. 1942.

▷ THE EIGHTH WONDER OF THE WORLD

On October 17, 1917, a year after the collapse of the central span, the first train finally crossed the Pont de Québec. This cantilever bridge, briefly considered the eighth wonder of the world, attracted tourists and scientists alike. The steel structure connects the two shores one last time before the great river makes its way to the ocean, hundreds of kilometres away. 1919.

THE HONEYMOON

Sending off a couple on their honeymoon was both a family and a community event. Then, as now, well-wishers gathered to wave at the happy couple. 1925.

◁ **WATER DAMAGE**

One reason why the cost of building railways was so high was the expense involved in constructing the roadbed. When it was done poorly, the result could be catastrophic. While the Québec landscape was certainly less difficult than that encountered in northern Ontario and the Rockies, it was not without its challenges, evident in this photograph where the roadbed has been washed away.

△ **ABITIBI**

Settlement of the Abitibi region was a result of the construction of the Transcontinental railroad, its route passing through these vast, virgin forests. Settlement began in 1912 and increased over the years. The trains continually brought new settlers and prospectors. In seven years, 16 parishes were founded, 50,000 acres of land cleared and 12,000 people settled in Abitibi.

THE FIRST TRAIN

The arrival of the first train was cause for celebration in every town. Communities fought long and hard to secure their own railway connection, offering land, financial incentives and sometimes borrowing money to finance the railway extension. The enthusiasm contributed to the construction of miles of useless track throughout Québec and mountains of municipal debt. When the Lotbinière and Megantic Railway arrived in Deschaillons in November 1894, the town celebrated with a masquerade ball. The railway connected Deschaillons-sur-Saint-Laurent to the Grand Trunk main line at Lyster Station. 1894.

◁ **NATION BUILDING**

Building the Intercolonial was Canada's first major effort in nation building. Railways and politics were intertwined, if not inseparable, in 19th century Canada. In 1861, there were 555 miles of track in Québec. The 1860s saw extensive construction in the province. The Intercolonial, built at huge expense, was intended to bridge the political and geographic chasm between Central and Eastern Canada, bringing New Brunswick and Nova Scotia into the political union, but was an economic drain on the newly united colonies. c. 1869.

△ **GRACEFIELD**

Gracefield, in the Gatineau River valley, was just one of the many thousands of stations built along Québec railways. The railways went to great lengths to ensure that their stations were both functional and attractive. Long after the demise of train service, communities fought to save their stations. In many regions, the battle to save the train station was the first of many to preserve the community's architectural heritage. Many stations have been restored to become community centres or tourist information kiosks. Others have been moved and transformed into private residences. 1914.

Photo Credits

PAGE   SOURCE

2   Jean-Baptiste Dupuis – n⁰. 478, Musée du Bas-Saint-Laurent
3   Paul-Émile Martin – n⁰. 11, Musée du Bas-Saint-Laurent
5   From the collection of George A. Driscoll, Call number: P630, P14651
12   François Fleury, 1943. Centre d'archives de Québec, E6, S7, P16121
14   J.W. Michaud, 1948. Archives nationales du Québec, E6, S7, P64623
15   E.-L. Désilets, 1948. Centre d'archives de Québec, E6, S7, P67073
16   Fernand Dufour, 1943. Centre d'archives de Québec, E6, S7, P15505
18   Donat-C. Noiseux, 1942. Centre d'archives de Québec, E6, S7, P7512
19   Zénon Pagé, circa 1900. Centre d'archives de Québec, P322, S2, D3-1, P1
20   J.W. Michaud, 1950. Call number: E6, S7, P75585. Centre d'archives de Québec
21   O. Beaudouin, 1948. Archives nationales du Québec, E6, S7, P63275
22   Paul Carpentier, 1941. Centre d'archives de Québec, E6, S7, P3644
23   Jean-Baptiste Dupuis – n⁰. 97, Musée du Bas-Saint-Laurent
24   Georges-Martin Zédé, 1909. Centre d'archives de Québec, P186, S2, D1-8, P76
25   François Fleury, 1943. Centre d'archives de Québec, E6, S7, P13732
26   Paul Carpentier, 1943. Centre d'archives de Québec, E6, S7, P13010
27   Donat-C. Noiseux, 1942. Centre d'archives de Québec, E6, S7, P9833
28   Inventory of Natural Resources, 1943. Centre d'archives de Québec, E6, S7, P17635
29   Eugène Gagné, 1935. Centre d'archives de Québec, E6, S7, P2228
30   From the collection of George A. Driscoll. Call number: P630, P6451
31   Inventory of Natural Resources, 1943. Centre d'archives de Québec, E6, S7, P17571
32   Herménégilde Lavoie, 1942. Centre d'archives de Québec, E6, S7, P443
33   Unknown author, circa 1940. Centre d'archives de Québec, E9
34   Unknown author. Call number: P167//5. Centre d'archives de Rouyn-Noranda
35   Unknown author, 1913. Call number: E57, S1, PB-1-21. Centre d'archives de Québec
36   Jean-Baptiste Dupuis– n⁰. 333, Musée du Bas-Saint-Laurent
38   Marie-Alice Dumont – n⁰. 1548, Musée du Bas-Saint-Laurent
40   Marie-Alice Dumont – n⁰. 1549, Musée du Bas-Saint-Laurent
42   From the collection of George A. Driscoll. Call number: P630, P11051
43   From the collection of George A. Driscoll. Call number: P630, D21251, P1
44   From the collection of George A. Driscoll. Call number: P630, D27151, P1
45   From the collection of George A. Driscoll. Call number: P630, D25951, P1
46   Donat-C. Noiseux, 1943. Centre d'archives de Québec, E6, S7, P13655
47   Jean-Baptiste Dupuis – n⁰. 5, Musée du Bas-Saint-Laurent
48   Jean-Baptiste Dupuis – n⁰. 245, Musée du Bas-Saint-Laurent
49   From the collection of George A. Driscoll. Call number: P630, P33249
50   From the collection of George A. Driscoll. Call number: P630, D27050, P1
51   Marie-Alice Dumont – n⁰. 1546, Musée du Bas-Saint-Laurent
52   William Notman, 1894, McCord Museum of Canadian History, Notman Photographic Archives, II-107192 (detail)
53   Firmin Proulx, 1866. Musée François-Pilote, L.77.31.F(13)
54   Canadian National. Archives nationales du Québec, Call number: P428, DL160, P2
55   Canadian National. Archives nationales du Québec, Call number: P428, DL515, P29
56   O. Beaudouin, 1957. Archives nationales du Québec, Call number: E6, S7, P3948-57
57   P. Gingras, 1895. Archives nationales du Québec, Call number: P585, P114
58   Fonds François Pelletier et Hélène Landry
59   Paul-Émile Martin – n⁰. 48, Musée du Bas-Saint-Laurent
60   J.W. Michaud, 1949. Archives nationales du Québec, E6, S7, P68477
61   unknown author, 1946, Canadian Pacific Railway Archives, NS.7594
62   J.W. Michaud, 1950. Archives nationales du Québec, E6, S7, P75337

63	J.W. Michaud, 1949. Archives nationales du Québec, E6, S7, P68593
64	From the collection of George A. Driscoll, Call number: P630, D13751, P2
65	From the collection of George A. Driscoll, Call number: P630, D14551, P11
66	O. Beaudouin, 1957. Archives nationales du Québec, Call number: E6, S7, P3695-57
67	Marie-Alice Dumont – n°. 176, Musée du Bas-Saint-Laurent
68	Marie-Alice Dumont – n°. 7157, Musée du Bas-Saint-Laurent
70	Jos.-W. Michaud, 1946. Centre d'archives de Québec, E6, S7, P32064
71	From the collection of George A. Driscoll, Call number: P630, D17051, P2
72	From the collection of George A. Driscoll, Call number: P630, D21449, P1
73	O. Beaudouin, 1957. Archives nationales du Québec, Call number: E6, S7, P3960-57
74	Marie-Alice Dumont, Musée du Bas-Saint-Laurent
76	Jean-Baptiste Dupuis – n°. 279, Musée du Bas-Saint-Laurent
77	Marie-Alice Dumont – n°. 1552, Musée du Bas-Saint-Laurent
78	From the collection of George A. Driscoll, Call number: P630, D39051, P5
79	O. Beaudouin, 1952. Archives nationales du Québec, Call number: E6, S7, P94160
80	From the collection of George A. Driscoll, Call number: P630, D46851, P2
81	O. Beaudouin, 1950. Archives nationales du Québec, Call number: E6, S7, P78482
82	Jean-Baptiste Dupuis– n°. 75, Musée du Bas-Saint-Laurent
83	Jean-Baptiste Dupuis – n°. 400, Musée du Bas-Saint-Laurent
84	Jean-Baptiste Dupuis – n°. 645, Musée du Bas-Saint-Laurent
86	Zénon Pagé, circa 1900. Centre d'archives de Québec, P456, S2, D3, P22
87	From the collection of George A. Driscoll, Call number: P630, P15351
88	R. Fournier, 1946. Centre d'archives de Québec, E6, S7, P32663
89	O. Beaudouin, 1953. Archives nationales du Québec, Call number: E6, S7, P97175
90	Unknown author, circa 1900. Call number: P266-3.3, 39. Centre d'archives de Montréal.
91	Unknown author, circa 1900. Call number: P266-3.3, 36. Centre d'archives de Montréal.
92	From the collection of George A. Driscoll. Call number: P630, D15349, P11
93	L. Arcand, 1947. Archives nationales du Québec. Call number: E6, S7, P36532
94	Malak. Archives nationales du Québec, Call number: P428, DL861, P1
95	O. Beaudouin, 1950. Archives nationales du Québec, Call number: E6, S7, P76453
96	Unknown author, 1913. Call number: E57, S1, PB-1-8. Centre d'archives de Québec
98	L.-J. Boulet, 1945. Centre d'archives de Québec, E6, S7, P27793
99	Omer Beaudoin, 1949. Centre d'archives de Québec, E6, S7, P69448
100	R. Charuest, 1946. Centre d'archives de Québec, E6, S7, P33797
101	Roland L'Espérance, 1944. Centre d'archives de Québec, E6, S7, P23188
102	Neuville Bazin, 1948. Centre d'archives de Québec, E6, S7, P63707
103	Jos.-W. Michaud, 1951. Centre d'archives de Québec, E6, S7, P84923
104	From the collection of George A. Driscoll. Call number: P630, D9250, P1
105	From the collection of George A. Driscoll. Call number: P630, P21149
106	Unknown author. Library and Archives Canada, Agriculture Canada Collection, PA 132974
107	Unknown author, 1925. Private collection
108	Unknown author. Archives nationales du Québec, Call number: P428, DL431, P67
109	Unknown author. Archives nationales du Québec, Call number: P337, D10, P62
110	Jean-Baptiste Dupuis – n°. 271, Musée du Bas-Saint-Laurent
111	Hethrington. Archives nationales du Québec, Call number: E6, S8, P117
112	Jean-Baptiste Dupuis– n°. 446, Musée du Bas-Saint-Laurent
113	Jean-Baptiste Dupuis – n°. 256, Musée du Bas-Saint-Laurent
114	Marie-Alice Dumont – n°. 571 and 396, Musée du Bas-Saint-Laurent
115	William Notman and Son, 1926-1927. McCord Museum of Canadian History, Notman Photographic Archives, VIEW-24035 (detail)
116	Ulric Lavoie – no. 04472, Musée du Bas-Saint-Laurent

117   From the collection of George A. Driscoll. Call number: P630, D536, P1
118   Unknown author, circa 1940. Frères de l'Instruction chrétienne, Pointe-du-Lac
120   H.H. Black, circa 1935. From the collection of the Reford Family
121   William Notman, 1871. McCord Museum of Canadian History, Notman Photographic Archives, I-63632
122   William Notman and Son, 1896. McCord Museum of Canadian History, Notman Photographic Archives, II-116161 (detail)
123   William Notman and Son, 1895. McCord Museum of Canadian History, Notman Photographic Archives, II-111790
124   William Notman and Son, 1884. McCord Museum of Canadian History, Notman Photographic Archives, II-73818 (detail)
125   Unknown author, 1910. McCord Museum of Canadian History, Notman Photographic Archives, MP-0000.848.4 (detail)
126   William Notman, 1869-1870. McCord Museum of Canadian History, Notman Photographic Archives, N-1978.109.1 (detail)
127   Paul-Émile Martin – nᵒ. 46, Musée du Bas-Saint-Laurent
128   McGill University, CAC 102036
129   Miller Services Ltd. Archives nationales du Québec. Call number: P428, DL826, P1
130   From the collection of George A. Driscoll. Call number: P630, P25551
131   Unknown author. Archives nationales du Québec. Call number: P428, DL900, P17
132   H. Lavoie, 1942. Archives nationales du Québec. Call number: E6, S7, P8246
133   Hethrington. Archives nationales du Québec. Call number: E6, S8, P171
134   Unknown author, circa 1890. Library and Archives Canada, Andrew Merrilees Collection, PA-165587
135   Unknown author, 1905. Library and Archives Canada, Andrew Merrilees Collection, PA-164716
136   Canadian Pacific. Archives nationales du Québec. Call number: P428, DL512, P1
137   Ulric Lavoie – nᵒ. 10910, Musée du Bas-Saint-Laurent
138   From the Collection of the Bartlett Morgan Family, 1919
139   William Notman and Son, circa 1921. Private collection (detail)
140   William Notman and Sons, 1911. McCord Museum of Canadian History, Notman Photographic Archives, II-187325 (detail)
141   William Notman and Son, circa 1921. McCord Museum of Canadian History, Notman Photographic Archives, VIEW-20016
142   William Notman and Son, 1890. McCord Museum of Canadian History, Notman Photographic Archives, VIEW-2350
143   Private collection
144   Unknown author, 1955. Call number: P25//114. Centre d'archives de Rouyn-Noranda
145   Antonio Pelletier, Musée du Bas-Saint-Laurent
146   L.-P. Vallée. Archives nationales du Québec. Call number: E6, S8, P467
147   P. Gingras, 1895. Archives nationales du Québec. Call number: P585, P105
148   From the collection of George A. Driscoll. Call number: P630, P65049
149   From the collection of George A. Driscoll. Call number: P630, P32749
150   Hethrington. Archives nationales du Québec. Call number: E6, S8, P41
151   William Notman and Son, 1901. McCord Museum of Canadian History, Notman Photographic Archives, II-136538
152   Antonio Pelletier, Musée du Bas-Saint-Laurent
153   Jean-Baptiste Dupuis – nᵒ. 52, Musée du Bas-Saint-Laurent
154   Jean-Baptiste Dupuis – nᵒ. 298, Musée du Bas-Saint-Laurent
155   Ulric Lavoie – nᵒ. 942, Musée du Bas-Saint-Laurent
156   Paul-Émile Martin – nᵒ. 28, Musée du Bas-Saint-Laurent
157   P. Carpentier, 1951. Archives nationales du Québec. Call number: E6, S7, P84893
158   Paul-Émile Martin – nᵒ. 44, Musée du Bas-Saint-Laurent
159   From the collection of George A. Driscoll, Call number: P630, D8449, P1
160   William Notman and Son, 1910. McCord Museum of Canadian History, Notman Photographic Archives, II-181632 (detail)
161   Marie-Alice Dumont – nᵒ. 5520, Musée du Bas-Saint-Laurent
162   Musée du Québec, fonds Edgar-Gariépy, box 94, nᵒ 11
163   Unknown author, 1910. McCord Museum of Canadian History, Notman Photographic Archives, MP-1021.17 (detail)
164   Canadian Centre for Architecture, 2.02/311.1
165   William Notman and Son, 1901. McCord Museum of Canadian History, Notman Photographic Archives, II-138781
166   Edgar Gariépy. McGill University, CAC 103156
167   Notman and Sandham, 1881. McCord Museum of Canadian History, Notman Photographic Archives, II-62288 (detail)
168   Jean-Baptiste Dupuis– nᵒ. 141, Musée du Bas-Saint-Laurent
169   Stanislas Belle – nᵒ. 14644, Musée du Bas-Saint-Laurent
170   William Notman and Son, 1910. McCord Museum of Canadian History, Notman Photographic Archives, VIEW-4856 (detail)
171   Jean-Baptiste Dupuis – nᵒ. 602, Musée du Bas-Saint-Laurent
172   Jean-Baptiste Dupuis – nᵒ. 12, Musée du Bas-Saint-Laurent
173   Jean-Baptiste Dupuis – nᵒ. 248, Musée du Bas-Saint-Laurent

174   Ulric Lavoie – no. 183, Musée du Bas-Saint-Laurent
175   Canadian National. Archives nationales du Québec. Call number: P428, DL515, P49
176   From the collection of George A. Driscoll. Call number: P630, D7249, P6
177   Stanislas Belle – no. 14468, Musée du Bas-Saint-Laurent
178   J.-Maurice Talbot, 1942. Centre d'archives de Québec, E6, S7, P5529
180   Alexander Henderson, 1870. McCord Museum of Canadian History, Notman Photographic Archives, MP-0000.10.141
181   Ulric Lavoie – no. 186, Musée du Bas-Saint-Laurent
182   From the collection of George A. Driscoll. Call number: P630, P57049
183   Paul-Émile Martin – no. 4, Musée du Bas-Saint-Laurent
184   Unknown author, 1900. Library and Archives Canada, Booth Family Collection, PA-120342
186   Jean-Baptiste Dupuis – no. 186, Musée du Bas-Saint-Laurent
188   From the collection of George A. Driscoll. Call number: P630, D528, P1
189   Paul-Émile Martin – no. 21, Musée du Bas-Saint-Laurent
190   Canadian National. Archives nationales du Québec. Call number: P428, DL102, P1
191   Canadian National. Archives nationales du Québec. Call number: P428, DL910, P1
192   Unknown author. Call number: P27-1512. Centre d'archives de Trois-Rivières
193   O. Beaudouin, 1957. Archives nationales du Québec, Call number: E6, S7, P1027-57
194   Unknown author. Call number: P5-156.1. Centre d'archives de Hull
195   Attributed to G. Martin-Zédé, 1906. Call number: P186, S2, D1, P471. Centre d'archives de Québec
196   Y. Couture, 1959. Call number: E6, S7, P2770-59H. Centre d'archives de Québec.
197   P.-É. Duplain, 1949. Call number: P322, S5, D6-1, P4. Centre d'archives de Québec
198   Unknown author, 1913. Call number: E57, S1, PB-1-22A. Centre d'archives de Québec
199   Unknown author, 1940. Call number: E9//10. Centre d'archives de Rouyn-Noranda
200   William Notman and Son, 1897. McCord Museum of Canadian History, Notman Photographic Archives, II-121,000.
201   Unknown author. Canada Science and Technology Museum/CN, Album H37.1, neg. 27557
202   A. Henderson. Archives nationales du Québec, Call number: P1000, S4, D36, P3
203   William Notman and Son, 1893. McCord Museum of Canadian History, Notman Photographic Archives, II-102021
204   Nicholas Morant, 1946. Canadian Pacific Railway Archives, M.3156
205   Unknown author, Canada Science and Technology Museum/CN, Album H09.2, neg. 31279
206   William Notman, 1859. National Gallery of Canada, (MBAC) 1993, p.80
207   Roger Robinson, 1951. Canadian Pacific Railway Archives, NS.25184
208   Omer Beaudoin, 1950. Centre d'archives de Québec, E6, S7, P77128
209   Ulric Lavoie– no. 1220, Musée du Bas-Saint-Laurent
210   O. Beaudouin, 1954. Archives nationales du Québec. Call number: E6, S7, P1251-54
211   G. Bédard, 1949. Archives nationales du Québec. Call number: E6, S7, P68278
212   Ulric Lavoie – no. 2979, Musée du Bas-Saint-Laurent
213   Unknown author. Archives nationales du Québec. Call number: P337, D10, P59
214   E.L. Désilets, 1949. Archives nationales du Québec. Call number: E6, S7, P73787
216   Canadian Airways Limited, 1938. Centre d'archives de Québec, E21
217   Compagnie Aérienne Franco Canadienne, 1930. Call number: E21, SCAFC, PZ31
218   Unknown author, Fisheries and Oceans Canada / Canadian Coast Guard, Laurentian Mountains' region, GCC-L 1B-AVN-GE-12
220   c. 1890, Library and Archives Canada, C 22139
221   Ellison and Co., circa 1860. Library and Archives Canada, Misses Robinson's Collection, C 90138
222   Notman and Sandham, 1878. McCord Museum of Canadian History, Notman Photographic Archives, VIEW-841.0
223   Valentine, circa 1905. Archives nationales du Québec, Quebec City, P547, DL431Q1, P29
224   William James Topley, 1911. Library and Archives Canada, William James Topley Collection, Album 16, PA 10270
225   Unknown author, 1910. Library and Archives Canada, Dept. of Mines and Resources Collection, Album 31, C 9660
226   Alain Franck Collection
227   Unknown author. Musée maritime du Québec de L'Islet-sur-Mer, 80.26.66
228   Unknown author, 1906. Fisheries and Oceans Canada/Canadian Coast Guard, Laurentian Mountains' region, GCC-L 1B-AVN-1705-01
229   Unknown author, Fisheries and Oceans Canada/Canadian Coast Guard, Laurentian Mountains' region, GCC-L 1B-AVN-1770-04
230   H. Lavoie, 1941. Archives nationales du Québec. Call number: E6, S7, P317
231   E.L. Désilets, 1949. Archives nationales du Québec. Call number: E6, S7, P73830
232   From the collection of George A. Driscoll. Call number: P630, P52651
233   From the collection of George A. Driscoll. Call number: P630, P53451
234   Canadian National. Archives nationales du Québec. Call number: P428, DL918, P1

236   Antonio Pelletier, Musée du Bas-Saint-Laurent

238   P. Provencher. Call number: E6, P215. Centre d'archives de Québec

239   Canadian National. Archives nationales du Québec, Call number: P428, DL912, P9

240   P. Provencher. Call number: E6, P571. Centre d'archives de Québec

241   Canadian National. Archives nationales du Québec. Call number: P428, DL776, P1

242   J.-Adélard Boucher, Musée du Bas-Saint-Laurent

244   From the collection of George A. Driscoll. Call number: P630, P9550

245   Canadian National. Archives nationales du Québec. Call number: P428, DL833, P4

246   P.-É. Duplain, 1948. Call number: P322, S2, D10-1, P1. Centre d'archives de Québec

247   Stanislas Belle – nº. 5000, Musée du Bas-Saint-Laurent

248   Unknown author, 1942. Call number: E57, S1, PB-54-38. Centre d'archives de Québec

249   Unknown author. Call number: P666, S12, D6, P56. Centre d'archives de Chicoutimi

250   M. Proulx, 1934. Call number: E6, S7, P68313. Centre d'archives de Québec

251   M. Proulx, 1935. Call number: E6, S7, P68298. Centre d'archives de Québec

252   R. Delisle, 1946. Call number: E6, S7, P31678. Centre d'archives de Québec

253   J.W. Michaud, 1950. Call number: E6, S7, P78687. Centre d'archives de Québec

254   William James Topley, date unknown. Library and Archives Canada, William James Topley Collection, PA-012446

255   J.W. Michaud, 1944. Call number: E6, S7, P21267. Centre d'archives de Québec

256   Unknown author. Call number: P60, D3, P51. Centre d'archives de Chicoutimi

257   J.-E. Livernois, circa 1875. Call number: P560, S1, P116. Centre d'archives de Québec

258   William Notman, 1872. McCord Museum of Canadian History, Notman Photographic Archives, I-76317

259   Ellison and Co., circa 1860. Library and Archives Canada, Misses Robinson's Collection, C 90137

260   William Notman, 1872, McCord Museum of Canadian History, Notman Photographic Archives, I-76322

261   William Notman, 1872, McCord Museum of Canadian History, Notman Photographic Archives, I-76324

262   J.-E. Livernois, circa 1890. Call number: P560, S1, P51. Centre d'archives de Québec

263   Livernois. Archives nationales du Québec, P560, S2, P300284

264   P. Provencher, 1939. Call number: E6, P97A. Centre d'archives de Québec

265   Unknown author. Call number: P24//420. Centre d'archives de Rouyn-Noranda

266   Unknown author. Call number: P60, D2, P51. Centre d'archives de Chicoutimi

267   J.W. Michaud, 1944. Call number: E6, S7, P20097. Centre d'archives de Québec

268   F.X. Labelle, 1869. Library and Archives Canada, Sir Sandford Fleming Collection, C-017695

270   Unknown author, circa 1880. Call number: P666, S12, D6. Centre d'archives de Chicoutimi

271   Unknown author. Call number: E57, S1, PB-12-93. Centre d'archives de Québec

272   Unknown author, 1913. Call number: E57, S1, PB-1-10. Centre d'archives de Québec

273   Jean-Baptiste Dupuis – nº. 236, Musée du Bas-Saint-Laurent

274   William Notman and Son, circa 1916. McCord Museum of Canadian History, Notman Photographic Archives, VUE-6050

275   L.-P. Vallée, circa 1880. Call number: P1000, S4, D26, P1. Centre d'archives de Québec

276   J. W. Heckman, 1901. Canadian Pacific Railway Archives, A-1145

277   P.-É. Duplain, 1945. Call number: P322, S2, D2-1, P1. Centre d'archives de Québec

278   A. Henderson. Call number: P1000, S4, D36, P23. Archives nationales du Québec

279   Unknown author, 1895, Archives nationales du Québec, Quebec City, P1000, S4 (N80-11-29)

280   Unknown author, 1864. Library and Achives Canada, C-003286

281   Studio Vachon, Mégantic, 1917. Canadian Pacific Railway Archives, J.C. McCracken Collection, A.1072

282   Alexander Henderson, 1871-1875. Library and Archives Canada, Sir Sandford Fleming Collection, PA-022009

282   Alexander Henderson, 1871-1872. Library and Archives Canada, C-014113

284   Alexander Henderson, 1871-1875. Archives nationals du Canada, Sir Sandford Fleming Collection, PA-022012

285   Alexander Henderson, date unknown. Archives nationales du Québec, P1000, S4, D36, P8.8

286   Alexander Henderson, circa 1879. Library and Archives Canada, PA-149706

288   J.W. Michaud, 1942. Archives nationales du Québec. Call number: E6, S7, P7010

289   Paul-Émile Martin – nº. 59, Musée du Bas-Saint-Laurent

290   Unknown author, 1925. Archives nationales du Québec, centre d'archives de Montréal. Fonds Joseph Mercure, P267, S7, P369

292   Unknown author, Archives nationales du Québec. P547, S3, SS2, D13, P3

293   Canadian National. Call number: P213//319. Centre d'archives de Québec

294   Unknown author, 1894. Library and Archives Canada, Andrew Merrilees Collection, PA-135133

296   Alexander Henderson, circa 1869. McCord Museum of Canadian History, Notman Photographic Archives, MP-0000.1828.52

297   J.W. Heckman, 1914. Canadian Pacific Railway Archives, A.21236